The Transparent Leader

A Business Fable of Clear and Effective Leadership Communication

Steve Gladis, PhD

HRD Press, Inc. • Amherst • Massachusetts

Published by: HRD Press, Inc.
22 Amherst Road
Amherst, MA 01002
413-253-3488
800-822-2801 (U.S. and Canada)
413-253-3490 (fax)
www.hrdpress.com

ISBN 978-1-59996-173-6

Editorial services by Donna Gladis
Production services by Jean Miller
Cover design by Eileen Klockars

Disclaimer

To the staff and faculty at George Mason University, specifically to my colleagues in the Communication Department, for their dedication, support, and kindness over the years.

Table of Contents

Preface

In *The Medium Is the Message,* Marshall McLuhan, the well-known scholar of communications, said, "You cannot not communicate." If you read the works of Daniel Goleman (*Emotional Intelligence* and *Social Intelligence*) as well as the huge number of books on communications and on brain neuroscience research, you learn that we all are communicating — all the time. Indeed, communication changes the way we think and the way others think. If that communication comes from you — and you're a leader — it has even more power. In short, our communicated thoughts, and especially our emotions, are contagious — for better or for worse.

Leaders' emotions — like confidence, joy, fear, and anger — get communicated every day to everyone looking to them for direction. Leaders, especially those who happen to be teachers and parents, know this to be true without question. Consider a young child who runs and falls. She will look back at her parents for their interpretation — their emotional reaction to the fall. If the parent shows fear or even anguish, the child often starts to cry. However, if the parent starts to treat it as funny (if it is a nonthreatening fall) and starts to smile, even laughs, the child "catches" the parent's positive emotion. Thus, leaders have a responsibility to realize the significant contagious impact of their thoughts and emotions on the minds and thoughts of others. Over the years, I have taught leadership communication, conducted research in this field, practiced it in large and small organizations, and been an executive coach engaged with leaders in public, private, and government organizations. During that time, I've had the privilege of being trusted by many who have shared their natural hopes, desires, fears, and misgivings as leaders. At the same time, I've been able to write about my experiences both directly and indirectly in more than a dozen books. In a sense, leadership communication has been my life's work.

Recently, my friend Cathy Lange, who was conducting a leadership seminar, asked if she could interview me in front of the group of emerging young leaders, specifically about my top ten insights regarding leadership communication. So to prepare myself, I thought about all the research I've both read and conducted and the experiences I've had vis-à-vis leadership communication, and I developed my "top ten" list. Of course the validity of such a list depends on the person making the list and the reader's willingness to accept those thoughts. This particular list is not the result of a single piece of research, but rather the experiences of a lifetime of reading, teaching, observing, and writing.

Our interview before the emerging leaders stimulated me to produce a more lasting document—a book—for not only new and emerging leaders, but also for senior leaders, particularly those for whom such skills don't come quite as naturally as more technical specialties might. I titled the book *The Transparent Leader* because when leadership is done well through excellent communication, leaders become increasingly open and more transparent to those around them. Clear, honest writing and speaking ultimately communicate to others that we're men and women of good sense, good character, and goodwill—the very essence of what the great Greek philosopher Aristotle would call a person of high ethical standing—and one who is worthy of trust. Without trust, there is little a leader can accomplish. With trust, there is little a leader cannot accomplish.

I have chosen to use the genre known as a "business leadership fable" to present my top ten list of leadership communication tips. My choice is girded by the research of famed social scientist and Stanford professor Albert Bandura, who is best known for "vicarious learning" (also known as imitation, modeling, social, and observational learning). Bandura's research suggests that stories—either true or fictional but realistic—help people learn. Stories with the greatest impact on learning are those that link closely to the intended audience and show how persistent negative behaviors can result in negative outcomes but how replacing these behaviors creates a far better future for the "reformed" learner.

From this psychological/sociological basis emerges a story form of vicarious learning experience: the business leadership fable. Recall for yourself how most of us, as children, learned life lessons through fables such as "The Tortoise and the Hare" ("slow and steady wins the race") and "The Boy Who Cried Wolf" ("when liars tell the truth, no one believes them").

I hope you'll enjoy reading and discussing this business leadership fable, which focuses on a young female executive, Stephanie Marcus, as she navigates the challenging world of business. Fortunately for Steph, she meets Lou Donaldson at the gym where she works out daily. Lou acts as a friend, informal coach, and mentor as he guides Steph through the complicated business ecosystem in which she finds herself. As a result, Steph changes. She also learns what happened to Lou early in his career and in his life, which helps her fully appreciate his wisdom.

If you have any doubt about how enthralling and edifying such stories can be, consider how soap operas attract such large, faithful audiences, all of whom are trying to figure out their own lives through the fictitious but realistic lives of these "vicarious learning" shows. Also, consider why programs like Alcoholics Anonymous or

Weight Watchers are so effective. Certainly, it must be in large part due to the stories that reformed participants tell to others who, just like themselves, are trying to kick the habit. These stories teach through a form of vicarious learning.

As is true of any teaching or advice, the ultimate test of effectiveness comes from the reader's experience and intuition. The final say rests with the reader telling himself or herself, *yes, that not only makes sense, it's what I've experienced as well.* So, read on and assess. I hope you enjoy the journey.

Steve Gladis

Chapter 1

The First Workout

Skyles Gym at 16th and H Streets in Washington, DC, wasn't particularly crowded on that rainy Tuesday afternoon in May. At 29 years old with her short cropped blond hair and steel-blue eyes, Stephanie Marcus looked like she might be a professional athlete training for an upcoming competitive event. Her smooth, tanned skin glowed golden from the sweat she'd produced from her five-mile run on the treadmill. Defined muscles rippled across her shoulders, arms, and exposed abdomen — Steph was an athlete, and she always received a fair number of admiring stares, even if they only lasted a few seconds.

She wiped off the sweat with a towel and tuned her iPod to the next Darden Business School lecture she'd downloaded. As soon as she heard the dean introduce the CEO, Steph moved toward the free weights to complete her late-afternoon workout. Without pausing, she brushed by Lou Donaldson, a graying 59-year-old CEO of a Washington, DC, public relations company, Donaldson & Associates. Another regular who hit the gym at 4 P.M., Lou stood in front of the free weights, gazing into the mirrored wall at his stocky physique, not paying attention to much of anything, save curling his thin arms with ten-pound weights.

"Sorry about that," Lou said while stepping back to avoid being hit by the weight Steph pulled off the rack. With her iPod volume turned up high, she didn't notice her ID and keys falling to the mat-covered floor and under the weight rack. Lou spotted them, reached down, and turned toward Steph.

"Excuse me, miss, your keys…" Lou said.

Steph didn't hear Lou—she was focused on carrying the weights over to a nearby bench, where she began her routine with a kind of rigor that inspires or intimidates those less disciplined. He tried to get her attention again, and still she did not hear him.

Finally he tapped her right shoulder. She jumped.

"What the …!" she said as she pulled out her ear buds and sat upright.

Lou backed up. "Sorry, but you dropped your ID and keys under the weight rack," he said, offering them to Steph, who then immediately felt the now-empty pouch hooked to her waistband.

"What?…I mean, thanks."

"No problem," Lou said, turning back to his own weights, perched on a bench close by.

"I see you here pretty regularly. I'm Steph Marcus."

"Good to meet you. I'm Lou. Lou Donaldson."

"You work around here?"

"Yeah, I have a PR agency just down the street in the Delaware Building."

"I'm just across the street—working for D&D Executive Search Consultants."

"Heard good things about the company."

"Thanks," she said, looking at her watch. "Well, got to clean up and get back for another long night."

"Sorry to hear that. Good to meet you, Steph."

* * * * *

Over the next few months, Lou and Steph began to chat more regularly. Usually, it was Steph who would start the conversation and Lou who would listen. From their conversations, Lou learned that Steph had been a soccer player at Duke for a championship team and then had gone to the University of Virginia's Darden Business School's MBA for Executives program, after which she went to work at D&D, Dideon & Dottson, a prestigious boutique executive search firm in Washington, DC. A natural competitor, Steph wanted to become the youngest partner at the firm and was doing everything she could to make that happen.

One week, she didn't show for her workout on Thursday or Friday. The following Monday, Lou spotted Steph moving slowly. She skipped the weights and was doing some stretching when Lou made an excuse to walk by her.

"Hi," he said.

"Hey, Lou."

"Missed you last week."

"Rough week."

"Sorry about that."

"Got passed over for partner."

"Really, how so?"

Steph explained that she'd hit, no, she had *crushed* every goal she'd set since coming to the company four years ago. She'd been at the top of her class at Darden and done everything and much more than the guy the firm had promoted. The only difference was that he was Mr. Cool, a funny guy whom everyone liked. And it drove Steph crazy. She'd produced the numbers; this guy produced the entertainment. "All hat and no cattle," as the Texans say.

"Sounds frustrating. This ever happen to you before?" Lou asked.

"Have to think," she paused and looked up. "Yeah, once in high school—when I didn't get elected to president of my class." She paused. "And, come to think of it, also when I didn't get captain of the soccer team at Duke."

"What happened?" Lou said.

Steph told him about the election in high school. She had worked like a dog, gotten her political platform together months before her opponent. She'd not just debated him in the auditorium but pounded him into the ground like a nail—but again, he was a cool guy whom everyone liked. As for the soccer team, she'd been the first one on the field and the last one off. Great stats, but when it came time for the peer elections, a quiet, thoughtful senior named Emily got the job, which stunned Steph.

"You see any pattern?"

"Besides getting screwed by the system, no."

"So, you think it's the process—the system?"

"Honestly, that and the good-old-boys club."

"So, it was a coed team at Duke?"

"No, of course not—I meant the class president and partner thing."

"OK. Anything else that could have been going on apart from the good-old-boys network?" Lou turned around to grab his towel.

"Damned if I know," Steph said, slamming the weights back into the rack, much harder than necessary.

Lou swung around to see what caused the commotion. "Whoa! You scared me."

Steph turned toward the Women's Locker Room. "I get so friggin' angry."

Lou pulled out his ID case. "Hey, here's my card. Stop by one day for coffee. I'll show you around, and we can chat."

"Thanks," Steph said. She took the card and headed for the locker room.

"Hope it works out for you. See you soon," Lou said, turning back toward the weights he'd just taken from the rack.

"Yeah," she said, waving her hand without turning her head toward Lou.

* * * * *

Steph's anger at not being selected for partner turned into a nagging fear about her future with her company. So, two days later, Steph decided to take Lou up on his offer to stop by. Lou's not-so-modest office overlooked the White House from 16th Street. When she sat down in a comfortable leather chair across from Lou, now in a striped blue starched shirt and a red and blue print tie, she said, "Wow. Not bad, Lou. Not bad at all! Have you always been in public relations?"

"Most of my life. Also, I've done some organizational development work, which has helped me understand the companies I work with better. But PR has been my main focus , even back in the Marine Corps."

That comment led Steph to ask several follow-up questions. In that discussion, she learned that Lou had joined the Marines right after college when he was 22 years old. She had to pull the information out of him, but she found out that he'd been badly wounded and yet managed to save three other Marines from dying. After nearly a year of rehabilitation, he had begun to walk again. He had attended law school and practiced law. He'd gotten a congressional staffing position on Capitol Hill, and later, he'd taken a senior position in the White House. But within two years he'd quit that job and set up his own company.

"Wow! That's pretty amazing. But why did you quit the White House?"

Lou waited a moment before answering, then simply said, "Power."

"Power? I thought that was why most people wanted to be in the White House."

"Not me."

For the next 30 minutes, Steph peppered Lou with more questions. She was surprised with every revelation. She learned that Lou had gone to Harvard Law after Princeton and the Marines. He'd practiced law for a huge New York law firm for a few years, before leaving to work on Capitol Hill. Then after his stint at the White House, he dove into public relations and started his own firm, Donaldson Communications.

"You just quit politics like that—gave it all up?

He nodded.

"Amazing. So, was it worth it?"

"I'd say so."

"What about your family?"

At this question, Lou suddenly looked very serious. After what seemed like a long pause in the conversation, he said, "Hey, this is about your career. Let's talk about you. What's your story?"

That's all it took for Steph. She talked about school, soccer, grad school, and her desire to become a CEO of a Fortune 500 company one day. She was neither embarrassed nor hesitant about describing her big dreams. Power, fame, and money—that's what motivated her.

"Fair enough. So let's say you got it all tomorrow— power, fame, and money. Then what?"

"Well, I guess, more of the same!" she said, laughing.

"OK. Do you know anyone who has power, fame, and money?"

Steph paused to think, then quipped, "Entertainers and movie stars, for one."

"And based on what you've read about Britney Spears, Michael Jackson, Elvis Presley, and a host of others, you think they are or were happy?"

"Well, maybe not in the end. But along the way...."

"So, for you it's the trip?"

"I guess. What about you?"

"I'm not interested in all the noise and the ups and downs that come with fame or fortune."

As she looked out the window that framed the White House, the ultimate power symbol, she said, "Yeah, right. And what's all this stuff...the office on 16th Street?"

"I'll admit that when I got started in this business, it was about the show, the power trip, money, and the appearance of success."

"Aha, I knew it."

"Yeah, but I learned a lot about the corruption of STUFF."

Steph looked around the office. "Lou, this is *the* cleanest...and sparsest office I've ever seen," she said, looking at a clear desk and the walls, bare except for one picture — a beach with waves gently breaking on the shore. "Where's that?"

"Rehoboth Beach, Delaware."

"So why's it so important — I mean it's the only picture in your office," she said, looking again at the pristine walls.

"Our family used to vacation there every summer."

"Now you don't?"

"It's a long story. Sometime when we have more time, I'll explain it."

Chapter 2

Sweating by the Numbers

Alex Dideon had started D&D Executive Search, Steph's employer, more than 15 years ago with a Wharton Business School classmate and friend, Frank Dottson, who left the firm after the first five years to start his own solo executive search firm. Alex retained the D&D working name because the brand had become so powerful. At 5'6", Alex stood several inches below Steph when she wore heels, which she rarely did anymore.

"Look at these numbers!" Alex said as he stabbed his right index finger at the net figure for the month.

"Yeah, I know, but I..." Steph tried to respond but Alex interrupted her.

"No excuses! You know I hate them, Steph. I just want solutions."

"I know that revenue has taken a hit. Maybe the oil thing...who knows. Best we can do is control expenses while we look for more revenue."

"You sound like a bumper sticker...buy low and sell high!"

Steph flashed a locked-jaw stare at Alex. "You got something to say?" Alex said with his hands on his hips.

Steph lost it. "Darn right I do! I got plenty. For starters, if you had looked carefully at the data, you'd find that ALL the revenue dips came from Jack Sunderlin's department. You know, Jack, your golfing buddy, who you just promoted to partner. So, I'm kind of wondering why the golden boy isn't here to discuss his performance — or lack of it."

Alex's face flushed red, and then he hammered his fist on the desktop. "How dare you lecture me! I taught business analysis before you graduated from high school."

"Maybe you need to review your lecture notes. Because Jack's bleeding the company dry. He hasn't sold a search engagement without your direct help since he's been here. He's a damned leech. Don't you see that?!"

"That's enough. It's patently unfair. Jack's not here to defend himself."

"Fine, call him in and let's confront him with the numbers. I'm game."

"Steph, take a time out. We'll discuss this later."

"A time out? What the...! Is this a business or a daycare center? Let's settle this thing like adults. Get Jack in here now."

Alex stood up, marched around the desk toward the door, opened it, and motioned Steph out the door. "We'll talk about this later."

Steph flashed her pale, piercing ice-blue eyes at Alex with such a laser glare that he looked down as he waited for her to leave.

When Steph returned to her office, she slammed the door closed and threw her notebook at the wall with such force that it knocked down a favorite picture of her with her best soccer friend at Duke. The picture fell and the glass shattered from the impact.

When she got to her desk, she sat down in her chair and heard the crunch of glass under its rollers. She picked up her notebook, opened to the copy of the report, and pressed the four digits for Jack Sunderlin. The phone rang until it hit voicemail with Jack's all-too-pleasant message, "Hey, this is Jack, I'm out or on the phone, so leave me a message. I'll get back to you today. Thanks a lot for calling."

"Jack, this is Steph. Call me. Right away!," she said, and hung up.

Next, she walked down to the second floor, to the CFO's office, and asked his assistant to run her monthly numbers against Jack's in a side-by-side analysis for the past two years. Jack headed up the corporate government contracting (Gov-Con) executive search side, which in Washington, DC, was a give-away account due to the vast number of government contractors lining the Capital Beltway for the billions of dollars the federal government offered in lucrative contracts every year. The federal government contracting sector had been 70% of D&D's business until Steph came on board and took over association and nonprofit executive search. Over the last two years, she had managed to move the association business to now slightly more than 50% of D&D's overall portfolio.

Back in her office, Steph looked around and picked up the picture and twisted frame off the floor, then left and headed straight to the gym. After she changed clothes, Steph hit the weights and then got onto the treadmill. Near the end of her harder-than-usual run, Lou Donaldson walked in, waved at her, and worked his way onto the stationary bike. He got into an easy, comfortable pedaling rhythm and broke out his *New York Times*, leaning back, as if he were on his couch at home…no hurry, no sweat.

Soon Steph finished her workout, started toweling off, then walked over to Lou. "Well, you look comfortable," she said.

Her voice startled him as he dropped the paper low enough to look at her over his reading glasses. "Hey Steph, how you doing today?"

"Fine." But her tone was abrupt.

"That bad, huh"?

She nodded and moved onto the free weights. A few minutes later, Lou made it a point to perch on the bench right next to her, where he noticed that she was curling 15-pound weights at such a rapid pace that she finally could not lift her arms. Sweaty, angry, and near exhaustion, she panted and hung her head down like a boxer who'd just been pummeled and had taken respite in her corner to lick her wounds.

"What's up?"

"Not much."

"Doubt that."

There was a long pause, "I had a bad day at the office with my boss." She told Lou the entire story about the altercation she'd had with Alex about productivity and her disgust with her colleague, who obviously was being rated by an easier scale than she was. "It's the good-old-boy club, and I'm not a member...plain and simple."

"Ah, the good-old-boy club again."

"You got it."

"I've heard this before."

"Damn right!" she said, throwing her workout note-book at the mirror in front of her.

Lou got up slowly, went over to the base of the mirror, where the rubberized flooring met the floor-to-ceiling mir-rored wall, and picked up the splayed notebook. He care-fully unfolded a few sheets of paper that had gotten damaged from the outburst and slowly handed the notebook back to Steph without saying a word.

Finally, she said, "I'm sorry. I just get so angry."

Lou took some time to respond but then said, "Hey, it's OK to get angry. You just can't always communicate it."

"Huh?"

Lou looked down at his watch and then at Steph and said, "I'm sorry to have to cut this short, I really am, but I have a dinner meeting with my former partner, whom I haven't seen in a very long time. So, I've got to get going. Will I see you here next week?"

"Yeah, if I don't get fired for punching out my boss!"

Chapter 3

Taking the First Step

The next time Lou visited the gym, he was running late. By the time he arrived, Steph was leaving and nearly knocked him over as she headed out. "Whoa! And hello to you, too!" Lou said, bracing himself to get hit by this oncoming train.

"Oh, hey, Lou."

"You in a big hurry to get back to the office?"

"Actually, no. I'm not sure why I'm rushing. Just habit. I'm actually taking a couple of days off to collect my thoughts."

"Got time for a quick cup of coffee?"

She looked at her watch instinctively, then at Lou, and laughed.

When they had finally settled into a local Starbucks on 17th Street—Lou drinking his decaf grande drip coffee and Steph, her tall skim latte—he asked her, "So, how's it going?"

"Well, if you mean work, fair to poor. Now, if you mean my social life, I'd say that's poor to awful!"

Lou laughed and said, "I only wish you were more honest!"

"Hey, you asked."

"So, what's happening at work?"

"Things went from bad to worse."

"How so?"

"Alex called me into a meeting with Jack. A real set up—more like an ambush. Jack had all these charts and graphs up in Power Point—all of which I was seeing for the first time. Totally smoke and mirrors to cover his poor performance. As I began to sort through his BS and started to ask some hard questions, Alex cut me off."

"So, where do you stand?"

"I told Alex that I needed a few days off to think things over."

"Like what things?"

"Like if I want to stay around long term or not."

"What are your options?"

"Haven't thought that far in advance."

"Good idea then to take the time off to think it through."

"So, what do you think?"

"You really want to know? I'm a good old boy, you know."

"Precisely why I need to know what you'd do."

With that, Lou pulled out a three-by-five index card and wrote down five letters—N.I.S.A.Y.—and pushed the card over to her.

"NISAY? What's that, Japanese?"

"No, it's what I think about when things in business or my private life start getting bad. Gives me real perspective."

"I can't imagine you having a tough time—either in business or your private life."

"Shows how easily you're fooled."

"Really? So 'fess up."

"Not my turn. We're talking about you."

"So, are you going to tell me what NISAY means, or is this a guessing game?"

"OK. When I got back from combat in Vietnam, I took a high-pressure job with a consulting firm. The days were long and stressful. I began to lose all sense of perspective."

"I can identify with that," Steph said. She raised her eyebrows and took another sip of her latte.

Lou continued, "Then, one night I was lying in bed in my hotel room, consumed with what I had to do to keep my unreasonable, neurotic boss happy. Suddenly, I must have dozed off and dreamt that I was back in the jungle in Vietnam, a young scared second lieutenant. Bullets were flying, people were hurt and yelling, grenades exploding, and I was scrambling, trying to keep the platoon from being obliterated by a company of North Vietnam's regulars."

"Damn, Lou, I'm sorry…"

"No need. I woke up soaking wet. My pillow was literally sopping. So, I got up and went to the desk, pulled out a piece of hotel stationery, and wrote it down."

"What?"

"N.I.S.A.Y. — Nobody Is Shooting At You!"

"You got to help me out with this, Lou. Explain please."

"Look, let me make a few assumptions about your situation — if I may."

"Assume away," Steph said with a casual wave of her hand.

"You're feeling ambushed, put upon, treated unfairly."

"Pretty good, so far."

"The water seems to be coming in over the sides of the boat faster than you can bail it out, and you feel like you're about to be washed overboard."

"A bit dramatic, but yes. I do feel overwhelmed and surrounded by alligators."

"NISAY can help you put your situation into perspective, because… Nobody Is Shooting At You, " Lou said. He paused for a sip of coffee, then continued. "Look, for an entire year in combat, people were literally shooting at me…and trying, really trying hard, to kill me. You're in a much safer place. You need to keep that in mind when the fur starts flying. It's all artificial. Doesn't mean it's not important to you...just that tomorrow you'll wake up, have breakfast, and read the newspaper."

"Hmm, never thought about it like that."

"I have to remind myself constantly, but whenever I'm in a pinch, either professional or personal, I think NISAY."

"I get it. So instead of going to a happy place, you go to the worst place you've ever been and start from there!"

"Gives me perspective—helps when things are turned upside down. It's my starting point. From there I have my Top Ten List."

"What?"

"I've collected my Top Ten Tip List from years of working in public relations and having to communicate with people. Has to do with being a transparent leader."

As she finished a bit of coffee, Steph put her cup down on the table and said, "OK, I'll bite. What's a transparent leader?"

Lou went on to explain to her in some detail his theory about leadership. He recounted his description of Col. A. J. Drummond, with whom he'd served in Vietnam. Drummond was a soft-spoken man who had an intensity that came from a deep respect for everyone he had ever encountered. He listened to all people—regardless of their rank—with the same level of attention as if they were generals. "You always walked away from a conversation with the Colonel feeling heard and understood," Lou said, "even as a second lieutenant—who just about nobody listened to, including the troops!"

"I know that feeling," Steph said, hitting the table with her hand.

Lou told the story about how the Colonel was planning to attack a large encampment of North Vietnam regulars (the country's army), the toughest bunch of fighters in the war. Well-equipped and professional—unlike the farmers-by-day and terrorists-by-night Vietcong—the NV regulars were seasoned, tough combat vets. The Colonel had planned on a predawn assault based on G-2 intelligence he'd received from Battalion Headquarters. However, a young second lieutenant, Matt Holder, who had led many a foray into the same territory, told the Colonel that it was a very bad idea.

"I won't forget his words: 'Sir, respectfully, Battalion doesn't know his elbow from a hole in the ground!'"

"I like this Holder already!"

Lou described how all the senior officers basically told Matt to shut up and listen, but instead the Colonel asked Matt to explain his basis for such a comment. Matt told him about the surrounding villages—and how the farmers acted as sentinels for the NV regulars at night until it was time for the farmers to hit the fields and harvest their rice crops—about a half hour after dawn. When the farmers left for the fields, the NV regulars were at their most vulnerable. The Colonel confirmed this with others at the meeting and changed his battle plan—all based on one outspoken lieutenant and a good listener—the Colonel.

"So what happened?"

"We caught the NVs with their pants down and, with almost no casualties on either side, we struck a decisive victory."

"So transparency is good listening?"

"Not just that, but it's a great place to start."

"Still not sure what transparency means here."

"It's openness. Letting others see inside and allowing yourself to see them—a kind of two-way mirror."

"You mean a piece of glass, then!"

Lou laughed, "Yes! When I'm honest and open with you, you will want to be the same way with me. It's only natural. When we both reflect that mutual loop of trust back and forth, it makes our relationship easier, faster, deeper, and more open — transparent."

"I get it, I think."

"Look, let's say you meet a guy at a bar, but he's very vague about what he does, where he lives, or much of anything — a very secretive sort of guy. What do you think?"

"He's married or already has a girlfiend!"

"Exactly, you think the worst case, this guy's not legit — he's holding back. You don't trust him. But, if he's open and honest, if he's transparent — a what-you-see-is-what-you-get kind of guy — your relationship has a chance to survive, even thrive."

"So, the same with transparent leadership?"

"Yep. And, like I said, I have my Top Ten Tip List for how to become an excellent transparent leader."

"OK, so let's have them."

"Not all at once — that would be like trying to eat an elephant at one sitting. But here's my first tip, and I think it might help you right now in your situation at work."

She had already turned over her brown Starbucks napkin on which she'd written N.I.S.A.Y. and had her pen at the ready. "Shoot."

"Listen first, then talk."

"OK, I'm listening, shoot."

"No, that was it — the first lesson of my Top Ten List. Listen first — then talk."

Steph laughed, shook her head, and wrote it down. When she'd finished, she looked up at Lou like he had two heads. "So, I guess you'll fill in the blanks?"

"Sure, it's simple. When you're talking, you are not taking in useful, vital information — you're only hearing what you already know."

"But how will someone know what you know if you don't talk?"

"Better to let them discover your brilliance than to tell them. An old writing professor at the University used to teach us to 'show, don't tell' the reader. Better to describe a guy kicking a cat in an alley than to say he wasn't fond of animals."

"Doesn't that take a long time?"

"In the short run but not in the long run."

"And this is going to help me with my boss how?"

"You might start by trying to listen carefully to learn what's really going on. Why is he so upset? What exactly does he want you to do? What would make him feel better? Emotions rule the roost. Find out the emotion that's below the surface, and you'll be on your way to solving the problem between you and someone else. You may be surprised if you asked him some questions instead of attacking him or his protégé."

"Damned twit!" she said, wrinkling up her face.

"That's what I'm talking about. You have to lose your anger, your negative attitude, and embrace the questions."

"Yeah, like how'd he become such a twit?"

"You're going to need some practice, I can tell."

With that, Steph wrote down the following on another Starbucks napkin:

The Transparent Leader— Top Ten List

1. Listen first, then talk.

Then she folded it and tucked into her wallet and said, "OK. Let me go practice listening!"

Chapter 4
Getting in Better "Listening" Shape

A couple of days later when Steph walked into Alex's office, he nearly flinched. She smiled and started the conversation by saying, "Alex, I've been doing a lot of thinking and wonder if I can ask you a few questions."

Alex put down his pen and said, "OK."

That opening question launched an hour-long conversation with Alex. He explained that he became concerned when several customers had confidentially told him that they felt as if Steph had steamrollered them into making purchases they weren't ready for. Eventually, one by one, each of them had shifted their accounts to a competitor—although they gave Steph plausible reasons why they were leaving.

Gritting her teeth, Steph continued to listen as Alex opened up and gave her greater detail, which eventually not only surprised her but also convinced her that what he said was true. By the end of this first listen-first-then-speak session, Steph was embarrassed and exhausted. She just thanked Alex for his candor and left. Surprisingly Alex smiled and thanked her!

Later that day, Steph called one of her former clients and asked if she could ask him a question. That led to another excellent conversation. Steph listened, and the former client explained some of his reservations and why he eventually left. Again, Steph was embarrassed and tired, but felt like she might be onto something. At the end of the conversation, she asked, "Is there anything I could do now to get your business back?" The client was so impressed that she had called and listened carefully that he suggested she stop by the following week — to give him time to think about the question.

Next, she called Jack Sunderlin and asked if she could come to his office for a few minutes. Jack paused but agreed to see her. When she entered Jack's office his arms were crossed, and he didn't get up but stayed behind his large desk.

Steph sat down and said, "Look, Jack, I know you've had some big successes with clients, so can I ask you a few questions?"

It took Jack a few seconds for her comments to penetrate his brain and transmit those comments to the locked arms clutching his chest. But when he did comprehend, he relaxed his grip. Putting his palms on the desk, Jack leaned forward and said, "Sure," as much in surprise as anything.

First, Steph asked, "Jack, why do you think you're so successful with clients?"

Jack pushed his hand through his long sandy brown hair and looked up to think for a bit. Then with an almost-embarrassed smile, he looked at Steph and said, "All my life, people have liked me."

"Liked you?"

"Yes. I think that's part of it...why clients stay with me. I'm likable."

"That's it?" Steph said, her voice rising slightly, as if on the verge of an outburst. But when she saw Jack start to recoil, she softened it to "Can you help me understand how that works?"

"First off I try to learn a lot about them — what they like. So, if they like to play golf or love to go deep sea fishing, when I'm with them I ask them to talk about what they enjoy ."

"Doesn't that seem artificial to them?"

"Not really. People love to talk about their grandkids, their boats, their golf games. It takes some time, but I'm genuinely interested and in the end, it makes a big difference. I get some touch points when they talk first."

"Touch points?"

"Sure, like one guy the other day talked about going fishing in Delaware—near Lewes. So happens that my family and I have vacationed at Bethany Beach for many years—so right away we've got a touch point—common ground. I'm already part way into his tribe."

"Tribe? What tribe?"

Jack explained that he was an anthropology minor in college. He'd become fascinated by the notion of tribes and studied them over the years. So he explained what he'd learned.

"We're all in tribes, any number of them. Take work, for example. When someone new gets hired and comes into the company, everyone tries to figure out whether this person will help or hurt the tribe. If the tribe sees benefit over time, the new person gets accepted and valued by the tribe. However, if there's any doubt, the tribe will keep the newcomer at arm's length. If the tribe senses a threat, it will reject or shun the newcomer, who eventually will leave or be rejected outright. Every tribe works pretty much the same way," he explained.

Steph listened but then asked, "So, correlate this for me to your business development?"

"Clients are tribes themselves. They're cautious about who they allow into their inner sanctum—especially outside vendors. Take D&D as an example. When a company decides to hire us, they're opening up their closest-held secrets. They tell us why the next executive position is open, who left it and why, and who they want to fill the new slot. It's like showing your blood work and x-rays to a stranger — your deepest secrets. They have to believe that you care about them and won't hurt them — won't hurt the tribe."

"And you do that how?"

"Look, I know I'm not as smart as you. I've read your résumé. But people like me because I listen to them, laugh at their jokes, and am sad for their losses. I'm certainly not an intellectual threat," Jack said, letting out a belly laugh. "But I'm really good at NOT creating resistance. I'm pretty much a friction-free, water–off-the-back-of-a-duck kind of guy."

Steph nodded as she made notes and drew a smiley face. She was beginning to understand and even like Jack herself.

Chapter 5

Getting into the Action

Skyles Gym was busier than ever on Friday. Many of the machines were humming, mostly with young men and women. Lou figured they were heading to the beach this summer afternoon and were buffing up before they hit the sand. He remembered those days.

Steph led the pack of sweating bodies on the elliptical machines. Later, hair soaked and a towel around her shoulders, Steph stopped by as Lou read the newspaper—the obituary section—and pedaled on his stationary bike.

"Lou, you're looking glum today."

"Yeah."

"We still on for coffee?"

"What?"

"Coffee—we still good to go today?"

"Coffee—oh, yeah. Right," he said, almost in a trance. He got off the bike and headed toward the shower, with the folded paper under his arm and his head down.

Steph sat at her usual table in the corner of the 17th Street Starbucks and was finishing up the day's first wave of e-mails on her BlackBerry®. She was checking out the front page of the *Washington Post* online when Lou came in still carrying the newspaper under his arm. He seemed to collapse rather than to sit down, and plopped down his coffee and paper on the table in front of him. He didn't speak for a minute or longer and just stared at the newspaper.

"What's going on?" Steph asked.

He pointed to a picture on the obituary page of a good-looking, middle-aged man with a broad smile. The headline said, *Sandy Osterman, Businessman and Philanthropist.*

"Sandy and I were partners back a long time ago when I was young and stupid. He was the guy I had dinner with a few weeks ago."

"Yeah, I remember you were going out with someone you'd worked with."

"We hadn't talked to any extent in over 25 years — mostly through our lawyers."

"Why?"

"I was stupid and stubborn. We'd been partners right out of graduate school. I was consumed with becoming wealthy, and Sandy just loved life...a fun guy. We got into a battle of styles, and he quit. He went on to start his own PR firm in Seattle and ironically became successful and very wealthy. So much so that he set up a large foundation to help veterans get back into society after war."

"Sounds like an interesting guy — a Vietnam Vet too?"

"Yep, he is — I mean was. He came back East to see a bunch of our friends and clear up some loose ends — like me."

"So how'd it go?"

"Really well. He was very sick. His doctor advised him not to fly, but of course, Sandy never listened, even to his doctor or his failing heart. We had dinner for four hours that night and ended up hugging each other and bawling on the street corner before he caught a cab back to his hotel."

"I'm so sorry, Lou."

"Me too. I was a jerk, and Sandy was as decent a guy as ever lived."

"You're a pretty decent guy yourself."

"Sure, just ask my wife...she'll....," he said as he clipped off the sentence.

"I wasn't sure you were married, Lou."

"Legally, yes."

"Oh, I see."

"Marion left me when..." he blurted out and then paused as he folded the newspaper and placed it at the edge of the table, "Marion left when our son Louis, Jr., was killed in Iraq."

"Oh, Lou, I'm so sorry."

"Louis was really a lot like my partner Sandy. He was carefree, easygoing. After 9/11, Louis and a group of his buddies joined the Marine Corps. Marion was dead against the idea. On the other hand, I actually thought it might teach Louis some discipline. So, while I didn't encourage it, I didn't discourage it either. When Louis died from a roadside improvised explosive device, Marion lost it. She blamed me and moved out less than six months later. That was two years ago, and I've been trying to patch it up since then — with little success. I've resigned myself to it and haven't seen her in about a year."

"Lou, I'm as sorry as I can be."

"I didn't really mean to unload on you." He got up from the table. "I'm not in the mood for much else today," he said. "Maybe we can get together early next week. I want to catch up with you — just not now."

Steph stood too and gave Lou a hug.

* * * * *

The following week, Steph and Lou sat at the same table. Lou had returned to his old self after a tough week. "So, tell me about how the meeting with Alex went."

"Seems like a long time ago now," she said, and went on to explain how well the exchange had gone not only with Alex but also with Jack. She told Lou how her opinion about Jack had changed, having heard him discuss tribes and anthropology. "Who knew!" she said, recounting how stunned she was to find out that Jack actually knew anything other than the baseball box scores.

"So, you learned something by listening."

"A lot. In fact, I got a former customer to talk to me and did the same thing with him. Asked him a dozen questions. What could I have done better? What was he getting from his new search firm that we didn't supply? Finally, I even asked him what we could do to win back his business."

"Good for you. So, what did he say?"

"Mostly, he was never sure if our firm really cared about his firm's success as much as just getting our retainer fee. And when I asked him about getting back his business, he told me to keep doing what I was doing — talking to him and asking what he needed, not what I wanted."

"Interesting."

"Yeah, and guess what? Next week I meet with him to pitch them for next year's account."

"Wow!"

"We may not get the business, but at least he's letting us in the door."

"I'd say you've got more than a good chance at winning back his business."

"Got my fingers crossed," she said. And she pulled out a three-by-five file card that said

---

The Transparent Leader— Top Ten List

1. Listen first, then speak.

"Well, now, don't you look prepared!"

"I upgraded from the Starbucks napkin! So, what's the next Transparent Leader Top Ten tip?"

"I'm not going to make it so easy for you this time. You have to figure this one out yourself," Lou said, leaning forward in his seat.

"I'm game."

"I'm going to pick out three tables with people sitting at them in this Starbucks right now. I want you to tell me the story about each one. What's going on at each table?" Lou looked around and then said, "Try that table with the young man and woman to the right of the front door."

Steph saw a young man in his thirties reading the paper while a woman, who looked like she might be his wife, stared off into the distance drinking her coffee.

"I think maybe there could be trouble in that relation-ship? It's like they're spinning in two separate orbits—not in sync. Can't be sure, but that's my take on that one."

Lou nodded but said nothing and pointed to a man typing on a computer in a far corner of the store.

"He's got on headphones. He's writing. Not sure if it's work or something creative, but he's serious about it and doesn't want to be bothered...the headphones make that clear. Funny though, he's in a public place. Must like the public stimulation, but he wants isolation at the same time."

Finally, Lou pointed to the barista. While making the drinks, she was laughing and joking with the customers.

"That kid enjoys the work, or she's had way too much caffeine!"

With that, Lou burst out laughing and clapped his hands in praise of Steph's insights. "I'd say you're on the money all around. So, what's the lesson?"

"Starbucks is a slice-of-life place where all different kinds of people converge," she said.

"Could be," Lou glanced down at his watch and then at Steph. "Don't let me make this a drawn-out guessing game." He paused and then continued, "Here's the tip: Actions speak louder than words."

"Huh?"

"You were able to learn a lot about the people in this place just by looking around. People told you the truth, without ever speaking a word to you. All you had to do was look...closely."

"You're right. Of course, I knew that. But somehow now it's so clear."

"Making the unconscious more conscious. That's all it usually takes."

With that, Steph wrote on her note card, *Actions speak louder than words*, and added it to her Transparent Leader list.

The Transparent Leader— Top Ten List

1. Listen first, then speak.

2. Actions speak louder than words.

Chapter 6

Keeping Your Head in the Game

The next week zipped by. Lou's attendance at the gym had been more erratic. When he showed up on Wednesday, Steph corralled him to get coffee with her after their workout.

"So, how you feeling these days, Lou?"

"OK."

"Not exactly a ringing endorsement. So, what have you been up to?"

"I spoke to my psychologist."

"Really?"

"About talking to Marion, if only to resolve our...situation, one way or the other."

"And?"

Lou explained that he and the psychologist had talked for a double session to pull together a strategy, and that it had worked! Lou met with Marion for several hours later in the week. Their meeting ranged from coolness, to anger, to tears. Marion had said that perhaps divorce would make sense now. However, her tone betrayed her feelings, so Lou had asked her to not make any decisions and to meet again next month. So, they remained at about the same place in their relationship, but with a chance, however remote, of getting back together—at least that's what Lou's intuition told him.

"Great," said Steph, "That does sound a little hopeful. My fingers and toes are crossed for you both."

Lou smiled and asked, "Well, what about your presentation to the former client?"

Steph told him about how Alex and Jack had wanted to get involved with the presentation to her client because the account was vital to the company's revenue. At first she was angry, but then she resolved that a team effort made sense and carried a certain level of insurance with it. They'd practiced and rehearsed, but the practice sessions had been interrupted and fragmented. She was frustrated, but fortunately the client had been called out of town and rescheduled for later this week. They had some time to salvage the presentation, in her opinion. So, she asked if Lou had any suggestions.

"Just so happens, it's on my Top Ten List!"

"Why am I not surprised!"

"The best solution is to do like the old Kentucky farmer suggests." He paused, then looked at her. "Tell them what you're going to tell them; then, tell them; finally, tell them what you told them."

"Huh?"

"People need to hear information several times to actually understand and retain it. So, you want to give the audience an introduction: Tell them what you're going to tell them. Then give them the body or guts of the presentation: Tell them. Finally, give them a conclusion: Tell them what you told them."

"Ah, the same thing my high-school teacher told me to do in my essays."

"Yep, I never said this stuff was rocket science. But along the way, a lot of us forget the fundamentals."

"Not this time," Steph said. She pulled out her trusty index card and wrote: *Tell them what you're going to tell them....* on her Transparent Leader list.

The Transparent Leader— Top Ten List

1. Listen first, then speak.

2. Actions speak louder than words.

3. Tell them what you're going to tell them...

Chapter 7
Staying Ahead of the Curve

When Steph, Alex, and Jack showed up at the office of Steph's former client, Max Engle, Max looked at the entourage and said, "Oh, Steph, I thought only you were coming over for a chat. Please, let me get a larger room for us all to meet." With that they were ushered into a much more formal board room. While Jack scrambled to get the laptop connected, Alex swooped down on Max like a hawk. Steph looked at Max, who shot her a glance, as if to say "Save me!"

Steph stepped in between Alex and Max and suggested they all sit down and get started. Alex shot her a harsh glance, then went over to help Jack, which gave Steph a chance to say to Max in a soft voice, "I'm sorry, Max, I really wanted to come over myself. I apologize for this." He just looked at her and shrugged his shoulders.

* * * * *

Lou and his wife Marion met again, this time for breakfast. Lou was careful to let her have her first cup of coffee before much discussion. She'd never been a morning person until she got some caffeine in her, but this was the only time she could meet this week, and Lou wanted to keep the momentum going.

"So, I talked to a psychologist...," Lou said.

"YOU talked to a psychologist?"

"Actually, for the past six months."

"Really?" she said, brushing back her graying blond hair. Marion was petite, slim and dressed right out of Ann Taylor—tastefully and elegantly conservative.

"Yes, I like him a lot. We've been working out some things."

"I'm glad for you."

"Actually, as part of the process, he asked if you'd be willing to come to a session sometime."

"Oh, Lou, I'm not sure. I'm...I think we're well past that. I..."

"I don't want to push it. If you're not comfortable, I can wait. Maybe you'll feel better later...or not. Either way, I'm fine."

"Thanks. I'll need time to think about it," she said, looking at him with her large green-hazel eyes that had melted Lou's heart so many years ago.

They had a pleasant meal. Conversation was a bit strained after the opening question, but Lou recovered well, and they ended with Marion agreeing to another meeting in a couple of weeks.

* * * * *

Lou was already sitting at the table and reading the newspaper at Starbucks when Steph came over with her coffee. "How long have you been here?"

"Not long. Please sit," Lou said. "So, how'd the big presentation go?"

Steph held out her right hand and pointed her thumb straight down—as if she were in a movie about the Roman Empire, giving the kill sign to the gladiator in the ring.

"That well, huh!" Lou said with a smile. "So give me some details."

Steph described the onslaught of her team on poor Max Engle, who had expected something quite different and more personal. Instead, her entire gang rolled into Max's office like a bunch of unwanted relatives coming to stay for the weekend. Max had to find a special room, got badgered by Alex, and listened to Jack's incessant golf stories. Steph did explain, however, that she had organized the presentation into a beginning, middle, and end, and that Max had even commented on the clarity of the presentation — perhaps the only bright spot. But, Steph could tell from the time they arrived that poor Max was not happy and more than overwhelmed.

Steph said, "I put all that work into a great presentation only to have it washed out to sea. Honestly, Lou, I felt like I was neatly arranging deck chairs on the Titanic as it slid into the water!"

"Now that's quite an image. I'm sorry that you went to all that work, only to get your presentation hijacked," Lou replied.

"Hijacked! Yep, that's exactly right. And Max got kidnapped!"

Lou laughed.

"So, what the heck do I do?"

"Understand where and how people get their energy."

"What?"

"Look, people are different, very different. Some more different than others."

Grimacing, Steph said, "Lou, sounds like sheer genius to me!"

"Just hear me out. Carl Jung, a Swiss psychiatrist, figured this out in his research a long time ago."

"Yeah, I read about him in my intro psych course at the University. He and Freud split ways, right?"

"Yeah, they both went their own ways. Jung discovered that people's personalities were different, systematically and predictably. His breakthrough research developed into his now famous book, *The Theory of Personality.* "

"Yeah, didn't he have something to do with the Myers-Briggs thing?

"The Myers-Briggs Type Indicator."

"Yeah, that's it."

"Actually, Isabel Myers and her mother, Catherine Briggs, wanted to make Jung's research available to Americans. Myers and Briggs thought that if people understood each other better, wars and conflict would stop."

"Good luck on that one!" Steph said as she reached for her coffee.

"Yeah, I agree, but their work did a lot to help people understand individual differences. And, one of the key pieces of Jung's work had to do with how people get their energy."

"Like from chocolate or coffee!" Steph said and broke into a laugh.

Lou smiled, "More like how they get their psychic energy...their capacity to process thoughts and emotions."

"Hmm."

"Let's take your client. What's his name again?"

"Max."

"Yeah, Max. Now I don't know him, but I'm willing to wager that Max is what Jung would call an introvert—a person who gets his energy by being alone or with one or two other very trusted people."

"Sounds right. I've never seen him around big crowds."

"And you won't see him in a crowd either, if he has a choice in the matter. Introverts trust themselves more than anyone else. They do all their mental processing internally, maybe with another very trusted friend—but never with someone they recently met and don't know well. Just not their style," Lou said, reaching for his coffee.

"That's Max alright."

"Now take your two colleagues, Alex and Jack. Based on what you told me about them in the past, Jung would call them extraverts. They get their energy not internally but externally—from others around them. And for strong extraverts, it doesn't matter much who that other person is. Extraverts do all their mental processing externally—just the opposite of introverts."

"You hit the nail on the head."

"In fact, extraverts do their best thinking when they're talking, but introverts do their best thinking when they're—well, when they're thinking! So what happened when you mixed the one introvert with the two extraverts...Max with Alex and Jack?" Lou said, looking straight at her.

"Meltdown! Max withered as Alex and Jack talked poor Max to death."

Lou laughed out loud and hit the table with his hand. "Exactly, it's like oil and water. The best way to win Max back as a client is a one-on-one meeting with you and him, if he's willing to meet with you after being so badly burned."

"Only one way to find out—call him," Steph said, writing a reminder note on the back of a paper napkin.

"I suggest you send him an e-mail or a written note. It would be more to his liking than what he might perceive as a confrontational phone call. He's a bit raw right now. Go slow."

"Got it," she said, and amended the note on her napkin.

With that, Steph pulled out her note card and wrote on it *People are different,* adding it to her Transparent Leader list.

**The Transparent Leader—
Top Ten List**

1. Listen first, then speak.

2. Actions speak louder than words.

3. Tell them what you're going to tell them...

4. People are different.

Chapter 8

Warming Up

The next two weeks went by quickly for both Lou and Steph but for different reasons.

Lou had client-related travel to New York City. One of his oldest clients had moved his headquarters to the city, and once a year Lou personally went there as a favor to his client, who paid very generously for the visit. At dinner one night, Lou's client—Henrico Ramirez, CEO of HR Associates, a boutique international Hispanic consulting firm focusing on Latin America—told Lou that he was considering selling his business and asked Lou his opinion.

"I'm not sure I can answer that question for myself and my own business, let alone for you, Henrico."

"You and I are about the same age and unfortunately the same weight!" Henrico said, smiling at Lou.

Lou looked at his ever-expanding waist, despite his attempts at the gym. "I guess that's about right," he said. "So retire or go to a spa in Florida where they'll starve you into better health!"

Henrico burst into laughter and said, "My friend, I do miss not having you closer. I enjoy our time together. I told Maria that I wanted her and me to spend more time together as we got older, and here we are all of a sudden...older."

"You think you could gear down enough to go into full retirement?"

"Not sure, but I doubt it."

"Ever thought about starting a new business?"

After Henrico's reaction of utter disbelief at starting a new business at his age, Lou suggested that he consider

some options. He could sell his business back to his partners, put the money into a healthy retirement fund, then
open a solo practice firm that would not compete with his
old firm. Lou suggested that Henrico consider, as only one
option, taking an office outside the city, maybe in Princeton or Long Island, and commute in whenever he needed
or wanted the city's vibe.

After an hour of discussion, Henrico said, "As crazy as
that sounds, I'm going to think about it. Why don't we go
into business together?"

"There you go, not even retired and thinking about
expanding already!"

The two men laughed, but on his way back to the hotel
that night, Lou gave a lot of thought to the very advice
he'd so willingly dispensed to Henrico — retiring to a small,
even solo, practice.

* * * * *

Steph was spending much of her time pulling together
executive search proposals for several of her best clients.
Her workload had started to heat up, and she didn't really
know why — she was just happy with the unexpected uptick.

Meanwhile, she had sent a note to Max apologizing for
the onslaught, told him that she would like to talk to him,
and said that she would call soon. Later, while on her
afternoon treadmill runs at the gym, she'd been practicing
a low-key approach to the Max situation before calling him.

Finally that afternoon, she picked up the phone and
dialed his number. Her call went through the usual palace
guards at the company, including Max's special executive
assistant. Finally he picked up.

"Max Engle."

"Max, it's Steph Marcus."

"Yes, Steph?"

"Max, I wanted to talk about what happened a couple of weeks ago," she said slowly.

"OK."

"I'm very sorry for the way you were treated. That meeting wasn't my idea. So, I wanted to offer my sincerest apology."

Max accepted the apology cautiously, as he waited for the probable sales pitch to follow.

Instead, Steph said, "Thanks, I appreciate your allowing me to clear that up. Take good care, and I wish you good luck with your company's continued future success — goodbye."

Max was caught completely off guard and said, "Just a moment."

"OK."

"We haven't chosen our search firm for this year. I'd like to talk some more about your ideas — this time alone."

"Well, sure...of course," Steph said. This was her turn for surprises.

* * * * *

Lou was pedaling at his usual gentleman's pace on the exercise bike, with the fan turned on high and reading the *Wall Street Journal*. Steph stopped by, toweling off from what must have been a rigorous workout.

"Hey, Lou, how the heck are you? How was the trip?"

He patted his stomach and said, "Too good."

"Want to catch up later today at Starbucks?"

"Sure, I can do it after work, around 6:30."

"Great, see you then."

* * * * *

Steph got her favorite table and was sipping her latte when Lou plopped down, dropping his briefcase and newspaper to the floor with a thud that said *I'm exhausted!*

Lou talked about his friend Henrico and how it got him thinking. He also mentioned that he'd convinced his wife to meet with him and his psychologist. Reporting this news made Lou light up in a way Steph hadn't seen since she'd known him.

"Lou, that's great, really great. I hope it works out for the best."

Still beaming, Lou said he hoped for the same.

Steph told him about her phone encounter with Max and how shocked she was when he asked to see her.

"I'm not so surprised myself."

"Really?"

Lou went on to explain that when people feel like they can trust you, the business equation changes immediately. He explained to Steph that had she launched into a sales pitch after her apology, Max would have blown her off for good. It was all about being trustworthy. "Trust," he said, "is made up of several components: competence, character, and caring."

"That makes sense."

"But, you have to have all three—competence, character, and caring—to be trusted. If you're smart but unreliable or dishonest, or alternatively incompetent but honest and caring, neither equation works. You need all three to make the trust formula work. And I suspect that's what Max experienced when you called him. The key for you was that you didn't try to hustle him. You truly were concerned about the relationship and not about the sale—precisely what got you the sale."

"So do I feel another tip coming through here?"

"Right you do: Trust matters, a lot. With trust, there's not much people can't get done and quickly. Without trust, not much you can get done, no matter how much time or money you have."

Wasting no time, Steph wrote down on her note card: *Trust matters a lot.*

The Transparent Leader—
Top Ten List

1. Listen first, then speak.

2. Actions speak louder than words.

3. Tell them what you're going to tell them...

4. People are different.

5. Trust matters a lot.

Chapter 9

Game Time

The following week, Steph sat in Max Engle's office, and he spoke to her about his executive personnel requirements for the next year. After talking for some time, he opened up to Steph, much to her amazement. He explained that he intended to put in place a succession plan — including a likely successor to himself — to ensure that the company would stay sure-footed and would remain a reliable place to work for his employees, as well as a source of income for both Max and his wife in their retirement, sometime in the future.

Steph just took notes and listened intently, almost disbelieving that Max would be so frank about both his personal and professional intentions.

"I've had some employees working here for more than 25 years and want them well taken care of," he said. "At the same time, Ingrid and I need to think about our own future."

"Can you describe the type of person you think might be the best fit to one day follow you as the leader of the company?"

So Max told Steph in specific detail the education, work experience, and social skills he looked for in his successor. To her surprise, he thought that someone who was more strategic and forward thinking, someone less like himself, might be the better fit during this next stage of the company. His honesty throughout the process was both flattering and helpful to Steph.

The meeting lasted for more than two hours, and Max did most of the talking.

* * * * *

Lou was already seated in his psychologist's waiting room when his wife Marion walked in. He stood and offered her a kiss on the cheek, which she accepted. When the receptionist saw that Marion had arrived, she told Lou that the doctor would see them now.

Dr. Nesbit sat in a large comfortable chair with a notepad resting on the arm of the chair. He rose when Lou and Marion entered.

The three of them exchanged greetings, then Lou and Marion sat down on the couch in front of a coffee table and the doctor took his usual chair. "So, we're here to discuss your relationship. Who would like to start?"

Marion looked at her handbag, but Lou looked at the doctor and said, "I guess I will."

Lou had practiced this opening many times. He was as factual and unemotional as possible as he described what the doctor and his wife already knew—the history of his son's joining the Marine Corps and his subsequent death in Iraq. But as he told the story in full detail and described his son's funeral, Lou's eyes welled up with tears that streamed down his cheeks. Without saying a word, Marion reached for the tissues on the coffee table and gently put one in Lou's left hand.

When Lou finished speaking, the doctor turned to Marion and asked her to describe what the past year had been like for her. She started where Lou had left off, at the funeral. For her that last year had been one very bad day after the next. She had blamed Lou for her son's death— plain and simple. She knew in her mind it wasn't rational, but that was how she honestly felt. She knew that if Lou had told their son not to go into the Marines, Louis might not have enlisted and would still be alive today. When she finished, Marion folded her hands in her lap.

"Fair enough," said the psychologist. "Lou, is there anything you want to say to Marion?"

Lou turned toward Marion and said, "Yes, I want to tell you, sweetheart, how heartbroken I have been this past year. But more than that, how much I apologize for not listening to you about the war." His voice trembled. "I was wrong, and it cost our son his life." As he spoke those last few words, Lou covered his face with both hands and broke into more a wail than a cry. It was as if everything he'd felt for the past year roiling inside him had erupted like an emotional volcano.

By then, Marion, too, was crying and had put her arms around Lou and pulled him close.

* * * * *

Steph couldn't wait to tell Lou how the meeting with Max had gone, so she called him on his cell phone. When he answered, she blurted out, "Lou, you were right. The solo meeting worked perfectly. Max opened up completely. Honestly, it was an amazing meeting, and I only said a dozen words."

"That's terrific. I'm so pleased for you and for Max."

Steph explained that she had not only gotten out her apology but also that Max had shared his personal and professional desires for the future. It was apparent to her that Max really wanted to secure his and the company's future and that he trusted Steph enough to help him.

"And, how'd it go with your wife?" Steph asked, almost apologetically, after she'd purged herself.

Lou shared the generalities about the emotional meeting with his wife at the psychologist's office. He purposely left out how they'd both broken down. But he did say how grateful he was that Marion had agreed to the meeting that was so painful for both of them. "The pathos was overwhelming," Lou said.

"What?" Steph asked, not sure what she'd heard.

"Pathos — the emotion that Aristotle talked about."

"The Greek philosopher?"

"Yeah, that's the guy. In personal situations — like yours with Max or me with Marion — it's never about the logical argument but about the emotion involved."

"I never thought of it that way."

"My favorite quote on that is from Teddy Roosevelt. He put it this way, 'Nobody cares how much you know until they know how much you care!'"

"Say that again, so I can write it down on my card!"

Lou repeated the quote, and Steph wrote it on her card: *Nobody cares how much you know until they know how much you care.*

The Transparent Leader— Top Ten List

1. Listen first, then speak.

2. Actions speak louder than words.

3. Tell them what you're going to tell them...

4. People are different.

5. Trust matters a lot.

6. Nobody cares how much you know until they know how much you care.

Chapter 10

Getting a Fitness Coach

When Steph told Alex about her meeting with Max and how he had opened up to her and basically promised her the business, Alex was ecstatic and high-fived her. But that buzz only lasted for a few moments. It was then that Steph told him how much Max had been offended by the way he'd been treated when Alex had insisted that he and Jack be in on the original briefing that had done so much damage to D&D's corporate credibility, at least with Max.

"I was merely trying to show Max the full range of our capabilities."

"I understand. However, Max is such an introverted man that meetings like that overwhelm him."

"But, if he only understood…"

Steph cut Alex off, "Look it's not the client's job to understand us. It's the other way around."

"Now what, you're going to start to lecture me about client management?"

"Alex, look, I'm just saying…"

This time, he cut her off. "Let's just end this discussion here."

Steph shook her head and walked out.

* * * * *

Starbucks was empty. The mid-afternoon crush had not quite hit. Lou had agreed to meet Steph earlier than usual because of the frustration in her voice. In fact, she was already there when he arrived. When he got his coffee, he sat down and said, "So, what's going on?"

Steph launched into a fast-paced, high-pitched description of her meeting with Alex. "Lou, I was so mad at him, I could spit. He doesn't get it...he is absolutely clueless. I'm just not sure how much more nuttiness I can take."

"OK. Let's sort this out. So, you're saying that Alex doesn't see how his actions upset the client."

"Right."

"Furthermore, he somehow thinks it's your fault?"

"I'm really not sure. But I'm very uncomfortable about our relationship. Can you help give me some direction?"

"I'm not sure, but it sounds to me like you have a culture clash. And the best way to begin to change that or any such problem is through a meeting of the minds. To accomplish a starting place for such discussions, I usually do a 360-degree assessment about whoever or whatever I'm dealing with."

"But I thought you were a PR guy," Steph said, reaching for her latte.

"My old organizational development skills have helped me a lot as I try to understand clients in order to help them project a better public image of who they are."

"Interesting."

Lou went on to describe the way he approached almost any such culture change situation. Specifically, he told her about the "four magic questions" that always open a door to discovery and further discussion. "So, in this case, the questions concerning the company's culture or climate might be worded this way." And he wrote the questions on a Starbucks napkin like this:

1. What's working well that we should CONTINUE to do?

2. What's not working well that we should STOP doing?

3. What should we START doing to improve things?

4. Is there ANYTHING ELSE you'd like to comment on that hasn't been addressed with the first three questions?

Steph reached for the napkin, looked it over, and asked, "That's it? Those four questions — those are the magic questions?"

"Yep," said Lou leaning back and taking a sip of his coffee.

With as much sarcasm as inquiry, Steph asked, "Really?"

"I'm hearing in your voice that you're doubting that these will work."

"Frankly, yes."

So, Lou told her to think about her last boyfriend. Steph rolled her eyes but agreed to play along. She recalled Luke, whom she'd dated for almost a year. Lou asked her which behaviors Luke demonstrated that helped their relationship, the ones she'd tell him to continue to do.

She thought for a moment and said, "He was thoughtful and kind."

"So, if he were here right now, you'd tell him to keep being thoughtful and kind — it's working in our relationship."

"Yes, I'd say so — *was* working in our relationship."

"OK — *was* working. So, next question: What behavior did he demonstrate that hurt your relationship that you would tell him to stop doing?"

She hesitated for only a second this time and said, "Stop spending so much money, showing up late for everything, and drinking so much."

"OK, sounds like if he were here now, you'd have a few things to settle."

"Darned right."

"OK, moving on. Next question: What would you have him start to do to help the relationship?"

"Honestly, I think he should start by seeing a doctor for his health and a psychologist for his compulsive spending."

"I see. Did you ever tell him this?"

"Not really. We ended up fighting all the time over these issues, until neither of us could take it anymore."

"OK, final question: What else would you say that I didn't ask about that he should know?"

"I guess, he's a nice guy with good intentions, but everything gets clouded over by these problems, and unless he's willing to take some steps, he'll keep repeating them."

After this brief five-minute exchange, Lou asked her, "So, if you and Luke had gone through this process, say with a counselor well before your break up, do you think it might have helped?"

"Yes, I actually do — as long as he didn't have a chance to critique me!"

"That's the tough part…it's a two-way street. But in companies that have used it, if everyone's willing to play honestly, it raises the elephant in the room.

"So, is this yet another of your top ten tips?" Steph made a motion to pull out the card she now always carried with her.

"Yep. It is."

And so Steph wrote down *To begin change, ask the four magic questions: continue, stop, start, anything else?*

The Transparent Leader— Top Ten List

1. Listen first, then speak.

2. Actions speak louder than words.

3. Tell them what you're going to tell them...

4. People are different.

5. Trust matters a lot.

6. Nobody cares how much you know until they know how much you care.

7. To begin change, ask the four magic questions: continue, stop, start, and anything else?

Chapter 11
Taking the First Step

Over the next two weeks, Steph met with Alex and Jack, separately and finally together, about her feedback from Max and how she thought they needed a fresh look at their company's approach to clients and public relations. Maybe, she suggested, it was also a good time to take stock of the corporate strategy as the company moves forward. That approach finally won over Alex, who liked strategic thinking — if only conceptually.

Once she got the buy-in, Steph suggested that the company engage Lou Donaldson's firm to help them work through this process. To do this, she showed Alex the long list of clients with whom Lou had worked and told Alex about how she'd known Lou for six months and found him an extraordinary resource who already knew some things about the company, just from his association with Steph. And while her honest revelations raised Alex's eyebrows, he agreed to meet with Lou over lunch to discuss moving forward. He asked Steph to set up the lunch, a lunch between Lou and Alex only. While Steph was unhappy about being left out of the discussion, she counted Alex's agreement to meet Lou a major victory.

* * * * *

The restaurant bustled with the noontime crowd, as Lou and the hostess approached Alex's table near the window. The two men greeted each other by shaking hands and introducing themselves, then they talked about traffic and the Nationals baseball team. As they ate their lunch, they finally slipped into the heart of the discussion.

"So, Lou, Steph tells me you're a strategy guru."

"She may have oversold me."

"She's done that before, but I suspect, based on what I've read about you online, that she's right on the money."

"Trust but verify," Lou said with a quick smile.

"Yes."

From that point the two men discussed Alex's concern with flat revenues and several lost customers—large ones. Lou asked a number of questions: Where was the company headed? What were the biggest blocks to success? And, did the company have an active strategic plan?

While Alex answered each question methodically, Lou watched him carefully, listened and asked follow-up questions, and summarized what Alex said to ensure that he understood Alex completely. Then he said rather matter-of-factly, "It seems to me by what you said that you have a clear interest in strategy—the future of the company, but aren't clear about the next steps. Is that in any way accurate?"

Alex took time to take a long sip from his iced tea, thought carefully, and then simply said, "Yes, that's accurate."

Lou asked a lot of other more operational questions—who were their top clients, what was their business development model, how did they recruit new talent, and did the company have strategic relationships with other firms?

As the two men drank a cup of coffee following the meal, Alex asked Lou if he had any interest in helping his company get some strategic direction.

"My inclination is to say yes; however, I have to think about it a while, especially the time commitment—given other things going on in my business and personal life."

"Well, I appreciate your honesty. Let me know in the next couple of weeks, so we can get started," Alex said.

"Or if you aren't interested, if you can give me a few names of other firms that might be interested, that would be helpful as well."

"Sounds good," said Lou, and the men parted with a handshake.

* * * * *

Later the following week, Marion and Lou were on what they had started calling "Date Night." Dr. Nesbit had suggested that perhaps a couple of times a month the couple could have a date centered on talking and getting reacquainted to explore their relationship. Lou had become very fond of their dates but didn't push Marion in the least. However, he did use her as his sounding board. This night they were at a French restaurant, which Lou knew Marion loved.

"So, Lou, what's going on in your business?" was all Marion had to ask, and Lou was off to the races. Mainly, however, he talked about Steph and her company, how he had considered them as a client but wasn't sure he wanted to mix friendship with business.

"What exactly does this Steph mean to you?" came the question from Marion, with a penetrating look. Lou knew her well enough to read this as thinly veiled jealousy, which made his heart leap. He thought within a second that if she were even the least bit jealous, there was room for hope.

"She's about the same age that Louis would be, and I thought I could help—that's all," he said as he reached over and took her hand and squeezed it. She squeezed back.

Chapter 12
Developing a Game Plan

Alex was pleased to get Lou's phone call a week after they'd had lunch. And a few days later, Lou met with the entire group — Alex, Jack and Steph — in the D&D conference room. Lou sat at the head of the table with a stack of index cards in front of him. After the introductions, the coffee and Danish, and some cordial banter, Lou suggested that they might want to get started. "Initially I'll be meeting with you twice a month, then once a month. That's the plan over the next year. We'll see how it goes."

Everyone nodded in assent.

"I like to do some exercises up front to help me, as much as you, understand the issues and the team. So, first off, I'd like to pass each of you four index cards." He asked them to write down the following four headers, one on each card:

Regarding the company's strategic planning:

1. What's working well that we should *continue* to do?

2. What's not working well that we should *stop* doing?

3. What's not working well that we should *start* doing to improve?

4. Is there anything else about the company's strategic planning process that you'd like to mention?

Then, Lou asked them to take about 10-15 minutes to fill out the cards but not to sign or print their names on the cards—he wanted straight, anonymous feedback. While they did so, he left the room and made a couple of calls, as much to give them privacy as to catch up with his other clients. When he returned, Lou took each of the cards and transferred the data to a flip chart, one sheet of paper per header, and stuck them on the front wall. There were only two points on the CONTINUE sheet:

- We talk about strategic planning every year at the management offsite.

- We had an outside speaker from the University speak to us. Might be good to get him back.

On the second sheet, there was nothing but the heading about what the team should STOP.

However, on the START sheet of paper, the list was longer and harsher:

- Let's get off the dime and DO something about strategy.
- Talk to experts.
- Hire a strategic coordinator.
- Make this happen, NOW.
- Involve our clients.
- Just do it.

On the ANYTHING ELSE sheet of paper, there were only two items:

- I'm glad Lou's here.
- Thanks, Lou.

After gazing at the lists, especially the "anything else" list, Alex said, "OK, Lou, did you stuff the ballot box?" The nervous laughs helped to cut the light tension in the room, and Lou laughed the loudest.

Next, Lou passed out another index card to each participant. "We'll talk about all these later, but on this card I'd like you to evaluate individually how you work together as a team on strategic issues. I'll give you statements for you to evaluate. Simply place a number next to each statement after you write it out. Rank them 1 to 5, with 1 meaning very low and 5 meaning very high:

1. How *do we now work* together as a team to be strategic in our business?

2. How *will we need to work* together as a team to become even more strategic in our business?

"Remember, no names please," Lou said as they started to write.

When the results came in, Lou aggregated them and then posted them on a separate sheet of paper:

1. We work together now: 2.5
2. We will need to work together: 4.5

There were some deep breaths from the group, some throat clearing, but Lou simply grabbed more cards and started passing out the next round — one card each. "On this card, I want you to list one, two, or three critical behaviors that *every* team member should change or modify to help us get from here to there — where we are as a team to where we want to be regarding the issue of strategic planning. Again, keep it anonymous."

When the results came in, Lou recorded and posted them dutifully:

1. Stop playing favorites.
2. Communicate honestly.

3. Share information.
4. Work AND play together.
5. Be open to change.
6. Resist the temptation to do nothing.

At this point, Lou asked the team members to prioritize the above list by giving each one a point value from one to five, with one meaning "low" and five meaning "high" in importance. They did this verbally, and he recorded the scores and then tallied them to pick the two clear winners:

Team Behaviors

- Communicate honestly.
- Share information.

Next, Lou passed out two index cards to everyone and asked them to put the names of the other two team members on those cards, one name per card. On one side, he asked them to *list three behavioral strengths of the person* and on the other side *two behavioral challenges that she or he needs to change* to get the team from here to there, regarding better strategic planning.

"Lou, can you give us a couple of examples of behaviors that need to change?" Alex asked.

"Sure," Lou said, "Maybe people have to listen better or procrastinate less or delegate a bit more, or perhaps not interrupt in meetings. Because you're all technically proficient at your jobs, you might want to focus your observations on social and interpersonal skills."

"Thanks, that helps."

When Lou stood up to go and get a drink of water, he could hear the group shifting their chairs and a throat clearing or two. He knew how difficult filling out these cards might be for them. And when he returned and collected the cards, he reviewed them and posted the results—to almost complete silence.

Individual Behavior Strengths

Alex
- Has great forward vision
- Knows his stuff

Jack
- Is liked by staff and clients
- Understands people very well

Steph
- Is the most focused person ever
- Is super productive

Individual Behavior Challenges

Alex
- Stop procrastinating with the strategic planning process.
- Listen better to others.
- Remember that everyone is different.
- Be careful not to try to take over clients.

Jack
- Take more responsibility and work more seriously—less like a fraternity.
- Pitch in when proposals are due.
- Stop talking behind people's backs.
- Stop saying "yes" to everyone when conflicts arise.

Steph
- Lighten up. Don't take work so seriously.
- Be more collegial — more part of the team.
- Stop complaining.
- Work together with others without having to control things.

After Lou wrote these out, the team members just seemed to stare at the feedback. "OK. Now, I want to take a 10-minute break so we can stretch, hit the bathrooms if needed, and also consider the feedback you have personally just gotten. When you return I'd like you to announce two behaviors that you'd be willing to change for the team to help the strategic planning process. Just two."

When all had returned and were seated, Lou stood and moved toward the lists now posted on the walls of the conference room. He carefully and slowly reviewed each list. First he addressed the "Continue-Stop-Start" list. After making fun of his own name being mentioned, he said, "It's very clear that the team thinks that strategic planning is important and that it hasn't been taking place as vigorously as everyone things it should. Is that a fair summary?"

The others nodded at varying speeds, Alex the slowest.

"How about the team ratings — 2.5 out of 5 for how you're doing now versus a 4.5 for what you'll have to do in the future if you want to become a team of strategic planners and implementers. Do you agree?"

Lou witnessed some shrugs but got general agreement from all present. Again, Alex was a bit slower to respond. Noting his reluctance, Lou said, "Alex, you all right with these numbers?"

Alex leaned forward and said, "I don't like being 2.5 out of 5. To me that means we're an F on an academic scale. I don't believe we're an F."

"OK, anyone want to respond?"

"I think it's just a scale for now. We haven't ever taken our corporate temperature. This is just a baseline," said Jack.

"I agree with Jack. I don't see it as a failure as much as a place to start," said Steph.

Alex still didn't look happy but said, "OK, but I still don't think we're an F."

"Fair enough," Lou said and moved on. "So can I get consensus that as a team you're not where you want to be and could stand some improvement?"

Everyone nodded.

Lou moved slowly to the next chart, allowing time for them to dissent or comment. Hearing and seeing none, he pointed to the list labeled "Team Behaviors."

"OK, here. From the list you all constructed, you chose two behaviors—to communicate honestly and to share information—as your top two critical behaviors that every team member needs to change to get the team from where you are now to where you want to be in the future to be more competitive in the marketplace. Do you all agree?"

The three colleagues looked over the lists and then nodded.

So, Lou moved to the other lists, which he suspected, based on his experience, might take some time. "Now, I'd like to discuss these last two charts—behavioral strengths and challenges. Let's do the strengths first."

Lou then went down the list, starting first with Alex and his vision and competence. Next, he commented on Jack's likeability and his ability to read clients, and finally about Steph's get-it-done productivity. All three of them smiled nervously as Lou described their strengths.

"Now, I want to describe this next list," Lou said, pointing at "behavioral challenges."

Alex spoke. "I need some info clarified before I can accurately comment," he said, with an edge in his voice. "For example, this 'taking over clients' comment." He looked at Steph.

There was dead silence for a moment. Both Steph and Jack stirred a bit, but then, surprisingly, Jack said, "Alex, frankly, you're a cool guy and you do always try to help us out. Sometimes that can come across like you don't trust us to handle things on our own. I think that's where that comment comes from."

Alex looked at Jack, then at Steph, who had to keep from high-fiving Jack. Then, Alex said, "OK. I guess I can see that."

For everyone there, the elephant in the room had been not only recognized but also properly introduced, and from that point forward, the discussion flowed with some tension but with a healthy air about it. Then, Lou asked all participants to take a few moments and pick two personal behaviors that they thought, if changed or modified, would help the team get to the next level of strategic planning.

Then, they reported — one by one. It took some time but by the time the discussion was over, Lou had established the following list, with everyone's agreement. The words and statements had been modified based on their discussion.

Individual Behaviors

Alex will

- Not procrastinate in developing and implementing the strategic planning process.
- Avoid interfering with clients unless needed or requested.

Jack will

- Be more seriously engaged at work.
- Stop saying "yes" just to be liked.

Steph will

- Lighten up and be more collegial.
- Stop trying to control everything.

After everyone agreed to these behaviors, Lou looked at the clock on the wall, turned to the group, and said, "This has been a terrific session as far as I'm concerned." He got some smiles and head nods. "We've been going hard for a couple of hours. I think we're at a good stopping point. So here's your homework and next steps." With that Lou outlined the following:

1. The team should meet regularly and should define what "regularly" will mean for them. In the beginning they could meet more frequently and then less so as time went on. However, they needed to start the planning process. To do so, they would also have to do their homework about the planning process, even hire a planning consultant if they needed that expertise.

2. Lou's role would be to work with them on how the team's behaviors were working in support of the process. He also agreed to help them facilitate the planning process — only as an "intelligent ignorant."

He explained the term as a smart process person who could ask good questions but who was not an expert in their business. Lou agreed to do this if the team were willing to do its homework on the strategic planning process.

They did agree, so Lou continued.

3. Initially the team would meet every two weeks with Lou for two hours and report their progress.

4. Every month each team member would solicit from the other team members a rating on how s/he was doing with the two team behaviors (communicating honestly and sharing information) and the two individual behaviors (which each had agreed on). Specific information would be solicited, especially if the behavior was not meeting the expectations and needs of the team.

5. Every three months, Lou would give them a survey instrument to rate the entire team qualitatively with a quantitative measure, but that would be explained later.

"Everyone OK with this for next steps?" Lou asked, looking around. All nodded. Lou smiled and said, "Let's get at it then! Oh, let me also add that if any of you want to talk to me individually between sessions, just give me a call or stop by — that's part of the deal."

* * * * *

A few days later, Lou and Steph were seated at their favorite Starbucks. She talked about all that had happened at D&D as a result of Lou's work with them. "I won't say it's been a miracle, but it's been a lot different. That's for sure."

"In what way?" Lou asked.

"Well, Alex is much more solicitous when offering his input on clients, and Jack is pushing back when we meet in conference. It's really funny to watch."

Lou smiled and asked, "How about you?"

"What about me?"

"How are your personal behavioral challenges coming?"

"Well, I…I'm working on them too."

"That's good. The lesson here is that people need feedback to find out where they were in the past, but that they also need feed-forward to find out where they need to go—to get from the past to the future. Look, I didn't make this stuff up myself. Marshall Goldsmith, the country's leading executive coach, came up with this and other processes to help teams. I'm just using them, with some modifications, to help you all out."

"So, should I write this feedback and feed-forward down on my tip list?"

"Sounds right to me, "Lou said.

Steph wrote down a note on her card: *People need feedback and feed-forward to get from the past to the future.*

The Transparent Leader—
Top Ten List

1. Listen first, then speak.

2. Actions speak louder than words.

3. Tell them what you're going to tell them...

4. People are different.

5. Trust matters a lot.

6. Nobody cares how much you know until they know how much you care.

7. To begin change, ask the four magic questions: continue, stop, start, and anything else?

8. People need feedback and feed-forward to get from past to future.

Chapter 13

Staying on Plan

The next two months were busy ones for the D&D team. Alex was committed to developing a new strategic plan and keeping it at the front of everyone's mind. To do so and to ensure that he kept himself on track as well, Alex listed his two key personal behaviors on a three-by-five index card, which he kept on his desk and took to every meeting. Steph and Jack were so impressed that they started to do the same.

At Jack's suggestion, the team had decided to begin with a SWOT model about internal Strengths and Weaknesses, as well as external Opportunities and Threats. Jack explained that the SWOT model for adaptation and change had originated at Stanford University from the work done by Albert Humphrey in the 1960s and 70s while using data and analysis from the Fortune 500.

Alex had asked Jack to lead the internal meetings — to show how much he trusted the process. And Jack accepted the responsibility, demonstrating how serious he was. At the same time, Steph tried to hang loose to help demonstrate her willingness to give up control. In all, they were all on their best behavior — sometimes falling off the wagon, only to be reminded by one or the other colleague about the "self-help" index cards right in front of them.

After their first meeting, they had several lists:

Strategic Planning—the next three years (SWOT exercise)

1. **Inside: D&D's *strengths* in executive search**
   - Quick response
   - Nimble, can change course quickly
   - Moderately priced and competitive
   - Lean expenses
   - Talented staff
   - Good client pipeline
   - High client retention rates

2. **Inside: D&D's *weaknesses* in executive search**
   - Lack personnel bandwidth to take on large clients
   - Small investment pool to expand
   - Sole proprietorship (Alex owns 100%)
   - Lack of advancement
   - Need better scope
   - Clients: lower level than what we should have

3. **Outside: The outside business environment *opportunities* for D&D's success**
   - D&D's biggest competitor losing its CEO and strategic direction.
   - The Regional Economic Development Office hiring a very dynamic CEO who is bringing a number of mid-level companies to the region— D&D's client sweet spot.
   - Alex being asked to become the chairperson of the local and powerful chamber of commerce.

4. **Outside: The outside business environment** *threats* **to D&D's success**
   - The soft economy.
   - Oil prices driving up corporate costs.
   - Two new executive search firms moving into town.
   - The renovation of D&D's building next year, which means we'll have to move out.
   - The negative press concerning another search firm, which was engaged in a lawsuit with a client (the bad press is hurting all the search firms in the area).

* * * * *

Steph and Max Engle had met several more times before she was eventually awarded the contract for a year. When that happened, Steph nearly jumped out of her skin. Alex was ecstatic for her big win. Personally tending to all the details of the account, Steph worked closely not only with Max's marketing manager but also with Max himself. As a result, their relationship grew stronger.

* * * * *

One day at a meeting at Starbucks, Lou and Steph talked about a wide array of topics. In the midst of this conversation, Steph said, "I just got an offer to be Max's Senior VP of HR."

"Wow. That's news. How do you feel about that?"

"Pretty good on several levels."

"Can you describe those levels?"

"First, getting Max back as a client was a major coup — I'm pretty proud of that. And, getting offered a corporate officer's position from Max gives my ego a huge boost."

"I'd say."

"Yes, and it sort of vindicates me to Alex."

"I see. Anything beyond that?"

Steph thought about it, and then shook her head.

Lou took a long sip of coffee. "Do you think there's anything left for you to learn from Alex?"

"Maybe."

"Not exactly a ringing endorsement."

"He's really trying hard these days."

The two went on to discuss the progress that the team had made. And while Steph felt like she could do some good things for the company, D&D's small size clearly inhibited her chances for advancement.

"Of the personal issues you pledged to work on for the team at D&D, do you feel like you've accomplished both?"

"Good question. Let me see. Hmm. Well, I think I'm doing better as a team player. Both Alex and Jack have commented to me independently that they've been very pleased with my performance and attitude overall."

"OK, sounds like a great place to start, but what about the two specifics and the team goals?"

"My gut tells me I'm doing fine, but I don't know exactly."

"So, how about if I move up the team evaluation a couple of weeks and you wait before making a decision? That would give me time to give you accurate scores, which might be very useful, whether you move on or not."

"Sure. That sounds like a good idea."

Chapter 14

Assessing Fitness

As promised, Lou announced that he would be conducting the team evaluation by e-mail, sending everyone their personal, confidential reports and then chatting with each team member privately. He also noted that every team member would get the aggregate team goal scores and any continue-start-stop comments about team goals as well.

Within the following week each team member received a Team Assessment Survey that looked like this one, although each was customized for individual participants:

Team Assessment Survey

Please rate (name of participant _____ Alex _____) on the following items. Place an X in the appropriate space below. A rating of 0 indicates no change in (participant's name) efforts to improve his/her leadership communication skills, -5 indicates great deterioration, and +5 indicates great improvement. First you'll rate him/her on Team Goals, next on Personal Goals.

Example:

(Participant name) is listening better:

-5__/ -4__/ -3__/ -2__/ -1__/ 0__/ +1__/ +2__/ +3__/ +4**X**/ +5__/

With respect to Team Goals (participant):

1. Communicates honestly:

-5__/ -4__/ -3__/ -2__/ -1__/ 0__/ +1__/ +2__/ +3__/ +4__/ +5__/

2. Shares information:

-5__/ -4__/ -3__/ -2__/ -1__/ 0__/ +1__/ +2__/ +3__/ +4__/ +5__/

With respect to Personal Goals (participant):

1. Does not procrastinate developing and implementing the strategic planning.

-5__/ -4__/ -3__/ -2__/ -1__/ 0__/ +1__/ +2__/ +3__/ +4__/ +5__/

2. Avoids interfering with clients unless needed or requested.

-5__/ -4__/ -3__/ -2__/ -1__/ 0__/ +1__/ +2__/ +3__/ +4__/ +5__/

Below, please provide a narrative answer or a list of your observations to the following questions regarding (participant's) Team and/or Personal Goals skills to date:

A. What does (participant) do well that he should CONTINUE to do to improve even more?

B. What should (participant) STOP doing to improve even more?

C. What should (participant) START doing to improve even more?

D. What other feedback do you have for (participant) regarding his communication skills?

Thanks for your cooperation.

Lou

Two weeks later, Lou sat in the conference room with the team reports in an envelope, and Alex, Jack, and Steph sat like college students awaiting their first graded essay in a freshman English class.

"OK. I have the results of the surveys."

There was a slight movement of Alex's chair. Steph just stared, and Jack made a nervous jot or two in his notebook. "First, let me make a comment. I'll give the aggregated team goal scores to you all with the comments as well. Then, I'll spend about 30 minutes with each of you to go over your individual scores. I'll start with Alex, then Jack, then Steph. Everyone OK with that?"

Everyone nodded.

Lou went on to explain how the team had rated "communicates honestly." With that he turned back a blank page on the flip chart to reveal the following information:

Communicates Honestly:

Team Goal #1 rating = 3.5 of a possible 5.0

Comments about that goal:

- We have to start telling bad news to each other along with good news.

- Let's stop looking at things with rose tinted glasses.

- Sometimes I think I'm not told the truth about my performance.

Then Lou flipped to the next page:

Shared Resources:

Team Goal #2 rating = 3.0 of a possible 5.0

Comments about that goal:

- We don't get resources evenly.

- Some are more equal than others.

- Sometimes I feel like stuff's being hoarded.

Lou let the information settle in. Alex spoke first. "Frankly I'm very disappointed," he said. "This basically shows that as a team we're C students in communication and D students in sharing!"

Lou explained to Alex what he had told him before — that this wasn't a test grade but an indicator of direction of progress, and that the team likely started at 1.0 in this area, thus had progressed farther than he realized. Alex nodded but was still not smiling.

"Any other comments?"

"I'd like to talk about sharing resources. It looks like we're all not happy about that one," said Jack.

With that, Steph spoke up. "Yes, I'm trying to conduct surveys of benchmarking companies," she said, "but I can't get any help from support personnel because they're too concerned with billable hours."

Then Alex jumped in. "Look, all this strategic planning is not bringing in any revenue—to pay salaries, for example," he complained. "So, I'm taking it out of my own hide."

Lou let the discussion go for a bit before reining it back in. "OK, so as a team, you all have got to talk about this sharing of resources more seriously in your weekly strategic planning sessions." They all nodded.

"OK. Any other questions?" asked Lou. He looked around and people were starting to gather their papers. "So, Alex, if you could stay here, we can chat about your personal progress. Jack, I'll give you a call when I'm ready to meet with you, probably in about 30 minutes."

After everyone had left, Alex turned to Lou and said, "This is not an easy process."

"Talking about the elephant in the room never is."

Lou then pulled out Alex's report and began to speak:

"I see some real progress here, Alex."

Alex smiled and pulled his chair closer to the conference table. Lou then explained that Alex had gotten scores of 3.0 in not procrastinating on implementing the strategic plan and had received a score of 3.5 in avoiding interfering with clients. This discussion went well because Alex now had a better understanding of what the numbers meant — a direction, rather than a be-all-end-all score.

After Alex, Jack came in, and he and Lou discussed his personal assessment. He had received a 3.5 in taking his work more seriously. "Wow, now does this mean I've gone over to the dark side?" Jack said, hitting the table and bellowing with laughter.

"I doubt you'll ever take life too seriously, so no danger there," Lou said, joining Jack in a good laugh.

They did discuss his 2.5 in saying "yes" when he didn't really mean it. Both he and Lou agreed that he needed to take on this goal as a real focus in his work.

Finally, it was Steph's turn to meet with Lou. "So give me the verdict, judge," she said as she sat down at the conference room table.

"Not guilty," Lou said without missing a beat.

Steph laughed, "Very good."

"So, let me begin with—well, lightening up." With that, Lou nodded to her and said, "The verdict is a 3."

"I'll take it, your honor."

Lou told her that he thought her score showed excellent progress. On the second item, controlling everything, she rated a 2.5, which Lou could tell disappointed her. "Look, you're making progress, but you and I both know that you do like to control things. So, this one's going to move more slowly. That said, your direction and the intensity shows me real, measurable progress. I'm proud of your progress."

"Thanks," she said, "I do feel like there's genuine movement in all of us."

"So have you given more thought to moving on to work with Max?"

"Yes, actually this process has helped me decide that— while by no means perfect, I'm ready to do that—take the job."

"OK. Let's just make sure you don't export your problem."

"Export the problem?" She raised her eyebrow and stared at Lou.

"Look—you, like all of us, have strengths—those abilities that come naturally, even easily, to you. You're smart, very logical, and analytical—to mention only a few strengths in your arsenal. And, we know that you try to control things. You have little tolerance for ambiguity."

"Darn right!" she said, as she hit the table and winked at Lou.

It took a second for the humor to register with Lou, but when it did he laughed hard. After a sip of water, he continued, "If you do decide to work for Max, I think you need to start out by engaging him to coach you by observing this trait that's hurt you in the past. It will take guts for you to mention it up front, but I know it will solidify your relationship with Max and your future with the company."

Steph agreed to every point her friend and mentor was making. And, Lou offered Steph his now almost patterned sailboat speech. He explained that simply put, great leaders — transparent leaders — start out like sailboats with a small leak in their hull. First off, they have to patch even the tiniest of holes, Lou explained; otherwise their boat would eventually sink. That's when he told Steph what she needed to continue to do with her control issues... patch them somehow, either by behavioral modification, proper staffing, or some other means she might use. Then, once those holes are patched in her "boat," she would need to hoist her largest sails — her strengths of intellect, determination, and drive. This two-step process — of stemming her challenges and focusing on her strengths — would ensure her future success. Lou explained that he'd rarely seen a problem with leaders that involved their basic professional competency, like accounting, law, or medicine. However, the complications arose in their leadership communication skills, or lack of them.

"Wait a minute," she said pulling out her dog-eared index card, "Is this another tip?"

"You broke the code," Lou said smiling.

Steph wrote down on her card: *Patch your challenges and lead with your strengths.*

The Transparent Leader— Top Ten List

1. Listen first, then speak.

2. Actions speak louder than words.

3. Tell them what you're going to tell them...

4. People are different.

5. Trust matters a lot.

6. Nobody cares how much you know until they know how much you care.

7. To begin change, ask the four magic questions: continue, stop, start, and anything else?

8. People need feedback and feed-forward to get from past to future.

9. Patch your challenges and lead with your strengths.

Chapter 15
Moving On

Under the direction and supervision of the therapist, Lou and his wife, Marion, had been "dating" now for several months. It had been a slow warming, but with Dr. Nesbit's guidance, Marion had softened her edge and opened up enough to have civil, even heartfelt, conversations with Lou about their shared tragedy.

Lou had come to examine his own motives in not having discouraged his son from joining the service and admitted that he had thought the experience would help Louis "become a man." Without hesitation, Lou had cried in front of his wife — something she'd rarely seen him do in his younger days, and that had signaled to her that Lou had changed.

Their "dating" continued and their fondness grew.

* * * * *

Within three months, Steph had given her resignation to Alex. This had gone surprisingly well. Because they were communicating so skillfully now, he had sensed she might be pulling away. Steph had taken a couple of weeks' vacation before she was to start her new job, and she felt ready to hit the ground running. Just before she reported to her new job with Max, she met with Lou at Starbucks for their usual chat.

"Well, you look tanned and fit," said Lou.

"Great vacation and had a chance to visit with my parents, but I started getting itchy to work after the first week off."

"So, when do you start officially?"

"Tomorrow."

"Wow."

"I can't wait to get in there and start making things happen, you know, mixing it up. I miss the action. The change."

Lou just listened and didn't respond too quickly to the energy force field sitting across from him.

"What's wrong?" she said, reading his nonverbals.

"If the president of the United States gets 100 days in office before he reports progress to Congress, why wouldn't you take at least that much time to get to know the situation you are in before changing it?"

"Huh?"

"Let's say a new roommate walked into your apartment and started to move the furniture around without consulting you. How would you feel?"

"She or he wouldn't be there too long."

"Precisely what happens to new leaders who go in without listening—the most important part of communication."

"Look, the reason that Max hired me was because I'm a get-it-done leader. I have a bias for action."

"I guarantee you that if you jump into a culture without knowing its origins and nuances, you'll create a backlash."

"But, my goal is to make the place better, more effective, and profitable."

"Slow and steady wins that race."

Lou went on to talk to her about spending most of the first month or two asking questions and mostly trying to understand—to read people's nonverbals, respect how people liked to communicate and basically build trust. Lou suggested that during those first three to four months,

Steph should only change things that were emergencies — and in such instances she needed to take swift action. But absent that, she would have to restrain herself from saying or doing too much too soon, without thoroughly understanding the situation.

"Listen, leadership communication is a discipline. You have to practice it every day to get good at it, just like being at the gym. In this case, it's the discipline of listening and NOT acting."

"But what about Max? What he expects from me?"

"Max wants you to be effective — long term. He's a smart guy. He also doesn't want the culture he's built to be damaged or threatened."

"What?"

"Culture is all the behaviors and beliefs of a particular social group — a tribe. In this case the group is Max's company. Your job is to figure out the tribal culture, get to know its subtleties, and then bend, not break it."

"Bend, don't break. Hmm."

"Cultures are like living organisms. When an outside foreign body approaches it, the organism or culture determines whether the new person or foreign body is friendly or hostile. If the culture sees you as hostile — wanting to change everything, just to put your mark on it or to control it — the corporate culture will surround, neutralize, and eventually kill the foreign body — you!"

"Hmm."

"Think about it. Don't you work the same way…don't we all? Who wants someone coming into our house for tea or coffee, telling us how to arrange our living room? Pretty presumptuous stuff, I'd say."

"Yeah, I guess you're right. But I'm more than a little concerned about what Max expects."

"So, ask him. Talk to him before you talk to anyone else. Tell him you want to learn about the corporate culture before you change or do anything. And see what he says."

"Good idea."

"I can't stress too much the need for being disciplined about this leadership communication. You have to think about it every day and act on it with discipline."

"So, is this yet another tip?"

"Yep, my last one. Communicating well is a discipline that takes effort. Like any skill, if you want to go from good to great, à la Jim Collins in his book *Good to Great*, you must develop a habit of discipline. Becoming a world-class listener, writer, speaker, team member, or leader demands sustained, directed, disciplined effort. It's like the guy who got into the cab in New York and asked the cab driver, "How do you get to Carnegie Hall?" The cabbie answered, "Practice, practice, practice!"

With that, Steph pulled out her card and completed the list: *Leadership communication is a discipline that needs to be practiced.*

The Transparent Leader— Top Ten List

1. Listen first, then speak.

2. Actions speak louder than words.

3. Tell them what you're going to tell them...

4. People are different.

5. Trust matters a lot.

6. Nobody cares how much you know until they know how much you care.

7. To begin change, ask the four magic questions: continue, stop, start, and anything else?

8. People need feedback and feed-forward to get from past to future.

9. Patch your challenges and lead with your strengths.

10. Leadership communication is a discipline that needs to be practiced.

Chapter 16
Epilogue

One year later, Lou and Marion celebrated renewing their marriage vows in a private ceremony at Rehoboth Beach in Delaware, where they had decided to retire. Actually, Lou opened a one-person PR office in Rehoboth, as a kind of lifestyle business; in fact the first picture he hung was the Rehoboth Beach picture, which used to hang on his DC office wall. And, Marion worked part time for a doctor's office. They bought a beautiful home in Henlopen Acres where they had often strolled when on vacation for the last 30 years. In a very real way, they had come home.

* * * * *

Alex and Jack formed a partnership, which had required the best from them both. Alex had to listen more to what Jack wanted, and Jack had to become more asser-tive about what he needed and wanted. So, it had been a delicate dance for more than one year, but the two had finally agreed on the partnership. What's more, Alex had suggested they change the name and rebrand their com-pany as DDS (Dixon, Dideon, and Sunderlin). Needless to say, Jack was overwhelmed by this gesture and accepted the offer.

* * * * *

Steph settled into her new position at the company. Max was relying on her more and more and had already decided to promote her to Executive Vice President. Fortu-nately, Lou had convinced Steph to hire an executive coach, which Max wholeheartedly supported and paid for.

Steph's coach had been a close friend of Lou's for years, one he'd used in his company at various points of both growth and challenge. Steph and her coach got along well and filled the gap created when Lou moved away. Steph's bumps along the road were not over, but with a coach Lou figured that she'd be able to avoid some of the larger potholes along the way.

To help herself remember all the tips Lou had taught her, Steph commissioned a plaque of the ten tips and hung it in her office. She also created a handout of the ten tips and gave it to all her internal associates, a number of whom she had started to coach.

The Transparent Leader— Top Ten List

1. Listen first, then speak.

2. Actions speak louder than words.

3. Tell them what you're going to tell them...

4. People are different.

5. Trust matters a lot.

6. Nobody cares how much you know until they know how much you care.

7. To begin change, ask the four magic questions: continue, stop, start, and anything else?

8. People need feedback and feed-forward to get from past to future.

9. Patch your challenges and lead with your strengths.

10. Leadership communication is a discipline that needs to be practiced.

Chapter 17

Leadership Communication

Today, many CEOs want their leaders to acquire what they sometimes call "soft skills," almost as if they see these skills as minor complements to more important hard skills. Certainly, for some people, math and science are indeed hard skills—especially people who aren't particularly good at those skills. However, the reverse is also true. Often, technically oriented professionals, who find accounting, law, math, medicine, and science easy, sometimes find interpersonal communication very "hard." So, never minimize the importance of communication skills, especially the leadership communication skills required by successful leaders. Such so-called "soft skills" have some very hard consequences when leaders don't possess and practice those skills.

So, why these particular leadership communication Top Ten Tips? The answer is relatively simple, even elegant. As I mentioned briefly in the preface, a friend wanted to interview me as a guest author for an emerging leaders program. I was feeling lazy and referred her to a recent book I had written called *The Journey of the Accidental Leader*, which had ten main leadership points—a neat fit, I thought. Fortunately, my friend read the book and said she wanted more communications-based advice—specific communications pointers for leaders. When I got her e-mail requesting that I focus more specifically on leadership communication, I gave her request some renewed thought.

To test myself, I considered all that I'd studied, researched, and written about leadership communication over the last several decades. Then, in 30 minutes, I wrote out a list: The Transparent Leader—Top Ten Tips. And that's how this book was born—sitting in my favorite coffee shop writing on a Saturday morning in Old Town Alexandria, Virginia.

I won't call this list a "dying declaration" of my professional truths, but pretty close. In fact, you could call the list my "Last Day Speech." By now, many people have heard of Professor Randy Pausch who had been invited by his university, Carnegie Mellon in Pittsburgh, to present his final lecture. This final lecture had become a tradition at that university, and once a year a professor was chosen to give his or her parting words of wisdom to a group of students and faculty before retiring. Randy's "last lecture" came with a twist—he was actually dying of cancer and only a very few close friends knew, surely not this entire audience. In fact, he introduced "the elephant in the room" in this lecture, which has since become one of the most downloaded videos on YouTube and which was made into a best-selling book. Regrettably, Randy has since died, but his memory and lecture continue to motivate.

I think my list is not so much my last lecture as it would be the speech I might give on my last day at work as I offered advice to young, emerging leaders before I hopped in the car to head for the tennis court. So here they are with commentary, my Top Ten Tips for excellent leadership communication.

1. Listen First, Then Speak

When people at work or at home come to us with problems, what's the natural tendency for just about anyone? If you said, "Give advice," you'd be right. Especially when you're more experienced and, worse yet, think you absolutely know the correct answer.

Unfortunately, unless the other person asks specifically for our advice, we make an error trying to offer it. The minute we start lecturing, we hijack the conversation. In a sense we steal the other person's cathartic moment. They don't get a chance to vent their story, which for many is all they really want—a listening, empathetic ear, not a talking head.

Stephen Covey and indeed St. Francis of Assisi talk about first seeking to understand and then seeking to be understood. Thus, in even a more direct confrontation—or face-to-face difference of opinion—you still are far better off asking questions and seeking to understand the other person's perspective first before offering your solution. By listening with a keen, here-and-now ear, you not only let the other person vent his/her feelings and emotions, but such listening also allows you to clearly understand the issue(s) and the intensity of emotion behind them. Thus, you can evaluate the facts and intensity of the issue before uttering a word.

You also gather background information, or what I call touch points, to which you can refer as you fashion a thoughtful response. For example, if in the conversation the person mentions that s/he used to work in Boston, when it's your turn to talk, you might want to say that you were born or went to school in Boston (assuming that were true). The more touch points you can collect by actively listening to the other person first, the more prepared you are to make yourself heard.

Avoiding a conversational hijack is critical for a single, powerful reason: Reciprocity. Virtually a universal value, reciprocity crosses cultures. If I give you something, there is an implied and compelling expectation for you to respond in kind, now or at sometime in the future, even the very distant future. To see how this works in everyday life, consider a conversation that you've had recently that you enjoyed. Chances are pretty good that in that conversation, the two of you took turns talking—in short, you both got equal amounts of "air time." Conversely, in a conversation where the other person drones on and on, never even seeming to take a breath, you likely left that conversation feeling flat and unheard. This lack of reciprocity in a conversation leaves people unfulfilled, even resentful. Listen first, then speak.

2. **Actions Speak Louder Than Words**

    One of the most compelling statistics I know to support this tip was offered by Dr. Albert Mehrabian, now professor emeritus at UCLA and leading researcher in nonverbal communications. Mehrabian discovered through experimentation something we all know innately, if subconsciously: Actions do tell the story. In fact, one of his principal discoveries is the following: Only 7% of communication comes from the actual words themselves, 38% is from the tone of the voice, and 55% comes from body language.

    If you consider tone as a form of nonverbal embellishment, Mehrabian's work is really saying that when we talk, only 7% comes from the words we speak BUT a whopping 93% comes from the way we say it—our nonverbals! This statistic provides a compelling tip: Observe others as they talk to you. In fact, you'd likely be better off if you could watch them communicating with the sound turned off to get an indication of their intensity and meaning.

There is a litany of nonverbals to watch for, and as we humans develop our forebrains, the prefrontal cortex, we learn how to interpret more what a person means than what he or she says. So, when I pass a coworker and say, "Hey, Jane, how's it going?" and she answers, "Fine," in a curt, clipped manner while forcing a smile, I know that things are anything but "fine" for Jane. At this point, if I'm inclined to be empathetic toward Jane, I might ask, "You want to talk?" or use some such opening to allow her to vent. You can bet that something's happened to her recently, and if you allow her to vent, she'll see that opportunity as a great gift.

So, nonverbals come in the tone of people's voices (sharp, clipped, pleasant, loud, soft); the way people stand (shoulders slumped, or straight back, arms akimbo or at their sides, an open or bladed stance); where they position themselves (close to you or at a distance); how they gesture with their arms and hands (large and expansive or confined and controlled); and finally, with some cultural differences, what they do with their eyes (look at you or away from you).

There are entire books written on the complete range of nonverbal communications, but no nonverbal is as important as eye contact. Certainly in many cultures, especially in the U.S., eye contact is viewed as a sign of honesty, a critical value in most societies for establishing interpersonal trust. Also, eye contact allows you to "listen" carefully with your eyes. Much like Jane, who said she was fine but showed by her nonverbals that she was not fine at all, people will often report something verbally that's inaccurate. And, it's important, especially as a leader, to pick up that disconnect. Conversely, to be heard and seen as a trustworthy speaker you must show others you respect them by looking at them when you speak. Thus, eye contact is an important two-lane highway for getting and giving feedback.

3. Tell Them What You're Going to Tell Them...

In his writings, Aristotle, the famous Greek philosopher and teacher, explained that people had to hear something several times before they really understood the message. His theory of rhetorical structure has survived and flourished for over the past 2,000 years—talk about a universal truth! Translated by an old Kentucky farmer, Aristotle's theory goes like this: Tell them what you're going to tell them; tell them; then, tell them what you told them.

Thus, whenever you speak to one or to 100 people—from a small informal briefing about a product or service, to a large formal speech about your industry and its future—basic rhetorical structure will create clarity for both you and your listeners. This key rhetorical structure consists of three parts: the introduction, the body, and the conclusion. Let's take each apart to help you better understand this key teaching by Aristotle, which still applies today.

The introduction of a rhetorical event (briefing, speech, testimony, even a significant conversation) gets the listener's attention. Using a short case history, some startling statistic, or even an example of how your service or product helped someone are all good ways of introducing your topic. Within the introduction, the next thing you'll want to do is explain how important your topic is to your immediate audience. Next, tell the audience your core argument (theme or thesis). This thesis, or central idea, literally controls and directs the speech. Most importantly, it tells the audience what you'll be talking about.

The body of the speech fulfills and supports the promise of the thesis. This section of the speech presents your several best arguments about why what you claim (your thesis or central idea) is true. Aristotle said that there were three ways to fulfill a claim of truth: ethos, logos, and pathos.

Ethos had to do with the speaker's credibility. Who you are and how you perform as a speaker have a lot to do with whether people will listen to or believe you. This point gets to the core of credibility. So, alluding subtly to your background and having someone of high esteem introduce you to the group help establish credibility, as does your general reputation in the community.

Pathos relates to how you might frame the critical arguments to support your thesis. Typically, pathos or emotional arguments are used when the audience is already philosophically close to the speaker...say at a political rally for a common candidate. Pathos appeals to the emotions of the crowd and can be used to motivate people into action. When you hear chants of praise or inducement you're hearing pathos ("What do we want? Change! When do we want it? Now!").

Logos represents scientific or factual truth, preferably from a credible third party. When you are addressing an audience that is neutral or that holds an opposite view of your thesis (for example, they are either for or against gun control), you must use hard, cold facts from a reliable and relevant source. And those facts should be marshaled from sources respected by the target audience. Here's an example:

"According to a recent story in the *Wall Street Journal....*"

The conclusion simply wraps up the speech. Again, because Aristotle established that people had to hear things several times to remember them, the conclusion is your last attempt to reinforce the thesis and your three main supporting arguments. Typically in conclusions, good briefers and speakers restate their thesis, review the three main arguments of the presentation, and then add a "closer" or final memorable statement at the end. This closer often looks like an opening statement and can, among other things, be a quote by someone famous or a call to action ("So, go out and vote for our candidate today!")

In short, tell them what you're going to tell them (the introduction); next, tell them (the body); then, tell them what you told them (the conclusion).

4. People Are Different

When I start a university class discussion with "People are different," everyone in the room looks at me as if to say, "Well of course." But what I'm talking about is that people are different in fundamental outlooks and how they get energized. The way people get their basic energy seems to be the most fundamental way their particular types operate in the world. In his seminal work, *Psychological Types,* Carl Jung explained that there are two fundamental energy types: introverts and extraverts.

Introverts get their psychic energy from being alone or with one or two other trusted friends or colleagues. After a tough week at the office, an introvert wants to crawl into a cave (a study, den, or basement) and read a book or watch TV—alone. Hibernating protects introverts from further depletion of their energy and lets them recharge for the next work week.

On the job, introverts prefer to work independently. They are self-directed and don't enjoy teams or lots of social small talk. Their most trusted advisors are themselves. In fact, when introverts come under stress, they become even more quiet and withdrawn as they pull deeply into themselves, thus foregoing interaction with others.

Introverts listen more and talk less, but when they do talk, they mean it. Unlike extraverts who talk a lot and use talk as a brainstorming exercise, introverts are very careful about the words they use. Introverts think before acting, they concentrate well, and they enjoy their internal life more than any other reality. For these reasons, ironically, extraverts are drawn to introverts — they give extraverts an audience!

Extraverts are very different cats than introverts. Whereas introverts draw their energy from themselves, extraverts draw their psychological wattage from being around others. And strong extraverts think that if one person is good, a group of people is even better. Primarily, extraverts get their energy and their best thinking when they're around others. So, at the end of a long week, an extravert gets energy at happy hour or at a party with a group of friends and colleagues.

Extraverts prefer to work with others because they use other people as sounding boards. They bounce ideas off their friends and colleagues to help them formulate and mold what they're really thinking. Because they're in almost a constant dialogue — even with themselves if no one else is around — extraverts speak often and well. They are among the most articulate and persuasive people, largely because they're practicing all the time.

Extraverts are broad-based thinkers with a wide interest in the world around them. They will talk to anyone, about anything, at anytime. They also enjoy and thrive in a team-based organization and often contribute significantly. Finally, extraverts enjoy the external world—that world beyond themselves. So, they can be very extraterritorial and walk around to other people's offices and cubicles a lot—especially seeking out good listeners like introverts!

5. Trust Matters, a Lot

Aristotle, who again is likely the wisest philosopher ever, talks about the importance of trust in his classic book *Rhetoric*. The book concerned itself with speakers—in his day, the orators in the Senate—a most important position in Greek society. Aristotle placed very high value on *ethos*, the credibility of the speaker. Ethos has been mentioned earlier, but it is so critical to trust—the core of any worthwhile relationship—that it needs to be discussed further.

Aristotle said that people (especially orators) were trustworthy if they possessed three characteristics: good sense, good moral character, and goodwill. Here they are simply put as questions: Did the speakers know what they were talking about? Were they honest and of good character? And did they have the best interest of others at heart? If one could answer yes to all three questions, then trust was built. Three simple, but very powerful, criteria: Good sense, good character, and goodwill.

Aristotle further explained that poor speakers easily form false opinions and become misinformed on any particular issue if they are not competent—in other words, they lacked good sense or mastery in their area of expertise. Or, such speakers could know the truth but be of such bad character that they would not tell it to the audience—they lacked good character. Or finally, they could know and understand the truth and even tell the truth to the audience but might manipulate such a truth to their own and not the audience's advantage—they lacked goodwill. Thus, good sense (being mentally competent); good character (being honest, fair, and balanced); and goodwill (having the best interest of another at heart) all work together to make leaders who will gain the trust of others.

Consider how this applies to your own relationships, particularly in business. If you're working with a brilliant colleague who often shades the truth to make himself or herself look better, it doesn't take long before you're double checking his or her reports. On the other hand, if you have colleagues who are honest and really care about you personally but are simply not knowledgeable or competent, it's impossible to trust what they have to say without verifying with someone more competent. This would be like your brother or sister calling you up with a great stock tip they overheard on the subway. "Trust but verify" would be the operative advice here.

Note that in high-trust organizations and relationships, many deals are done with a handshake. However, in low-trust relationships, it costs much more and takes far more time to lock in agreements. Such low-trust relationships call for lawyers—who get paid by the hour and apparently by the complexity of words they use. Thus, we pay far more for an untrusting relationship than we do for a trust-filled relationship. And, the transactions take a longer time to happen. In relationships — personal and business — trust is a show stopper or a show starter.

6. **"Nobody Cares How Much You Know Until They Know How Much You Care" (Teddy Roosevelt)**

The concept of "caring" relates directly back to what Aristotle said about goodwill. We tend to listen more closely to people who (we believe) care about us and our cause. You can see this basic instinct in animals or kids, the two best barometers of goodwill. Both are so viscerally oriented that they can literally smell your goodwill, animus, or fear.

In fact, our brains have an entire alarm system called the amygdala, which is a walnut-sized, reptilian, primitive brain within our larger brain. The amygdala signals us, when confronted by something unknown, to respond with flight, fight, or freeze (the-deer-in-the-headlights syndrome). This subconscious mechanism — the amygdala — is so highly attuned because of primitive survival instincts that such alarms happen in a fifth of a second — the amount of time that may allow us to survive or perish in a threatening situation.

A certain look on someone's face, a stance, or a whole array of nonverbal cues will signal the amygdala that something or someone isn't good for us (lacks goodwill) and thus should be avoided and mistrusted. And while the amygdala is not always accurate, it always errs on the side of caution. Thus, because our goodwill detector is so finely tuned (perhaps too finely tuned in some people — the highly anxious), at any hint of ill will or grandstanding, the amygdala hijacks the brain and tells it to exercise extreme caution. And when the bells and whistles go off, it's hard to undo them and start all over again, even when the amygdala is overreactive and wrong.

So, the caution here is to go out of your way to be a person of not only good sense and good character but also especially of goodwill. Going out of your way to establish goodwill might sound minor; however, such goodwill becomes central to having others allow you into their trusted inner circle. Thus, people don't care how smart you might be until they have confidence that you actually care about them. Teddy Roosevelt had it right: "Nobody cares how much you know until they know how much you care."

7. To Start Change, Ask the Four Magic Questions: Continue, Stop, Start, and Anything Else

Question: Whenever you're asked to evaluate any issue, where do you start?

Answer: With people who deal with the issue every day. However, leaders acting as evaluators most often start with themselves and what or who they know and thus develop a skewed view of an issue. For example, management may look at business expenses as a situation that's gotten out of control, but until they talk to line supervisors and salespeople dealing directly with the customer, they will never have a clear picture of the problem. So, the first approach to attacking a problem is to develop a 360-degree perspective. Talk to key people—those above, below, and at your same level, asking them about the issue.

Once you have identified the key stakeholders in this process, you will need to ask them some pointed questions. Remember that many of the people you will talk to may have a vested, even a heavily vested, interest in the topic or issue. Therefore, they could be defensive, perhaps protective, in their responses.

That's where the four magic questions come into play. I'm not sure of the origins of these four questions, which consultants have used perhaps since the beginning of self-reflection. I call them magic questions because they elicit such amazing answers, no matter what the issue. So here are the four questions again:

1. What are we currently doing well (regarding a particular issue or function) that we should CONTINUE to do to be successful?

2. What are we currently doing that we should STOP doing to be even more successful?

3. What are we currently not doing that we should START doing to be even more successful?

4. Is there ANYTHING ELSE relating to this topic you'd like to tell me that I didn't ask you?

In my experience, these four questions are great to ask if you want 360-degree feedback about any person, function, or issue that you want to assess and improve. The topic does not matter—these questions not only get to the core issues quickly, but they also do so while first honoring what people are doing right. This is why the first question is always: What are we currently doing well that we should CONTINUE to do to be successful?

8. People Need Feedback and Feed-Forward to Get from Past to Future

When people want to make progress in their professional relationships, good coaching begins with helping them develop self-awareness. And, the place to begin such self-discovery is with the 360-degree assessment process, which looks at how your boss, peers, and subordinates (your 360-degree universe at work) perceive your strengths and challenges.

There are many instruments available for this purpose, and the one I've most frequently used is the above-mentioned four questions: Continue-Stop-Start and anything else people want to mention. Information that you collect based on what a person has done in the past is called feedback. Naturally, the person being assessed can do nothing to change what he or she did in the past. So this feedback provides a kind of historical benchmark—a baseline—from which to move forward in his or her working relationships.

Typically, my clients provide eight to 10 names of people who know them well and whose feedback the clients respect. I then either interview these people or ask them to fill out a questionnaire, which I follow up on if I need clarification. Then I collate the data, remove any references that could identify anyone, and write a report that I present to the client. Often such reports are difficult for clients to read initially because they must come to grips with how they are perceived by their universe at work. I've yet to conduct one of these feedback sessions where there aren't some discovery or "aha" moments—both good and not so good.

Following such a baseline exercise, clients need some way to go forward. Marshall Goldsmith, the country's leading executive coach, has come up with a technique that many coaches, including me, now use: feed-forward. Simply put, feed-forward is a mechanism that allows people who are significant to the client (such as colleagues) to provide ongoing help with coaching those clients through personal, periodic discussions. In these discussions, colleagues provide tips about how the clients can do better at a specific challenge in the future (thus the term feed-forward). Then every several months, observing colleagues have an opportunity to provide a progress report to a neutral party—the coach—who collects, collates, and provides an updated evaluation to the client. This same sort of feed-forward information is important with teams because it rates how team members are doing on both team-related and personal behaviors, which are vital to team success.

9. Patch Your Challenges and Lead with Your Strengths

Every new client I accept gets my "sailboat analogy" the first time we meet. I used to draw a picture, but then started bringing in a small brass boat from my desk. It's a sleek two-masted sailboat about six inches long and four inches high. First, I explain that we all are like a sailboat, sometimes with a very small leak in the hull—really a pinprick of a leak. This kind of leak in people is their key challenge—the one challenge that, if they could patch it, would improve their performance—disproportionately for the better. It could be arrogance, micromanaging, abusive behavior (bullying), always needing to be right, and so on. Read

Marshall Goldsmith's new book, *What Got You Here Won't Get You There*, for an extensive list of such challenges. In any case, if this challenge or leak is not patched early enough in a leader's tenure, the hole in the hull will enlarge until it actually sinks the boat. So, we start here — with the challenge.

When the leak is patched through feedback and feed-forward and behavioral changes, we turn to the client's strengths. There are several instruments to help determine key strengths, not the least of which is a 360-degree evaluation and a self-assessment instrument like The StrengthsFinder (available online at www. strengthsfinder.com with the purchase of the Gallup publication *Now, Discover Your Strengths*). When people discover and confirm their primary strengths, they're ready to lead with them.

One note here: no one ever goes to the next level in a sport or in business by making their weaknesses their key focus. Rather, they improve most dramatically by making something they do well even better. The idea of going from good to great or even from great to best in the world resonates here. Of course, the process starts first with the challenge, then with the strength.

So as an example, if a client has difficulty communicating with others, we'll begin with that challenge and find ways to listen to how others might want to be informed (by e-mail, meetings, etc.) and how frequently they need to be updated (daily, weekly, monthly). When the feed-forward and the feedback on 360-degree follow-up assessments start coming back positively, then we focus on a key strength. Let's say that the client is very strategic. Then, we'll see how we can use that skill, perhaps in an upcoming corporate reorganization as well as in the company's strategic planning initiative.

To demonstrate this visually, I show the clients my two-mast sailboat again and explain that they have a definite strength that everyone (peers, direct reports, and bosses) recognizes. That's when I point to the larger of the two sails. Also, I show them that if we add a bit more to the boat's sail capacity, it moves even faster in the water. This simple sailboat analogy of strengths and challenges proves very effective, especially because I leave it on my desk so clients see it every time they come in for a coaching session—I believe it's that important.

10. Leadership Communication Is a Discipline that Needs To Be Practiced

In his book *Good to Great,* Jim Collins, like every sports coach I've ever had, talks about the absolute need for discipline. Here's a quick definition for discipline that I like, and I think you'll understand why when you read it:

> Discipline: *Activity, exercise, or a regimen that develops or improves a skill; training: A daily stint at the typewriter is excellent discipline for a writer.*

As I sit here at 6:23 A.M. typing away on my computer, I'm demonstrating a level of discipline. When you go for a walk or to the gym regularly, you're demonstrating discipline. When your boss shows up prepared for his meeting with a solid, well-thought-through agenda, s/he is showing discipline.

Any skill that you want to improve must be practiced in a disciplined way. Athletes, writers, dancers, doctors, lawyers—all know that discipline is at the core of greatness. Without it, you'll never get to the next level. And so it is with communication. To become an all-star communicator, you must practice communicating skillfully, and this practice must become a discipline, not a casual, hit-or-miss thing. When leadership communication is done well it looks effortless — much like how Tiger Woods hits a golf ball. He calmly walks to the tee-off area, inserts a tee with his ball on it. He measures with his club, then blasts a ball hundreds of yards straight down the fairway as if he were swatting a fly. But what we don't see are the hundreds of thousands of practice shots that he's hit on driving ranges, the coaches bearing down on him over time, and the playing in tournaments in rain and cold weather since he was a youngster.

Discipline is getting up in the morning, lacing up your running shoes, and hitting the pavement before anyone else has considered the idea. Discipline is staying at work to finish a tough proposal after others have long gone. Discipline is parents working with their child to help him read a story or finish his homework. Discipline is about sticking with something worth doing until it's done well. Indeed, if you want to get better at anything, you must do it yourself, not give it to a colleague or someone you hire. Tiger Woods can't rent someone to practice for him. Discipline in leadership communication is you staying at it each and every day. And the more you practice such leadership, the more transparent a leader you become...someone people can see through, someone with no hidden agenda, someone with a clear and a straightforward, honest manner. One who can be trusted.

For Further Reading

Buckingham, M., & Clifton, D. (2001). *Now, Discover Your Strengths.* New York: Free Press.

Collins, J. (2001). *Good to Great.* New York: Harper Collins.

Covey, S. (2004). *The 7 Habits of Highly Effective People.* New York: Free Press.

Goldsmith, M. (2007). *What Got You Here Won't Get You There.* New York: Hyperion.

Goldsmith, M., Lyons, L., et al. (2000). *Coaching for Leadership: How the World's Greatest Coaches Help Leaders Learn.* San Francisco: Jossey-Bass.

Jung, C. (1971). *Psychological Types.* Princeton, New Jersey: Princeton University Press.

Mehrabian, A. (1972). *Nonverbal Communication.* Chicago: Aldine-Atherton.

Other Books by Steve Gladis

The Executive Coach in the Corporate Forest (HRD Press, July 2008)

Foreword by Marshall Goldsmith, the world's leading executive coach. A business fable, *The Executive Coach in the Corporate Forest* is the story of a young, gifted executive coach, J. C. Williams, and his coaching relationships with his rather varied and interesting business clients—all with their own challenges. The book offers some engaging stories, has believable characters with realistic problems, and illustrates the structure and content of the coaching process. The book is a quick read and was written to explain the coaching process to executives who didn't understand it.

The Journey of the Accidental Leader (HRD Press, October 2007)

Written as a business fable, *The Journey of the Accidental Leader* is the story of a young man who, like so many people, gets thrust into a leadership position he neither wanted nor asked for. What he does and how he reacts makes the book both entertaining and informative. This book is based on the author's practical leadership experience as a Marine Corps officer in Vietnam.

Manager's Pocket Guide to Effective Writing (HRD Press, January 1999)

Written communication is prevalent at most levels of business, but especially at the managerial level. Your writing may be grammatically and logically sound, but is it effective? Is it conveying your message with the concision and accuracy that makes you an effective communicator? Whether you're a manager in charge of a group of writers, or just a person interested in improving his or her writing skills, *The Manager's Pocket Guide to Effective Writing* uses easy, practical, how-to steps to help you write better and ultimately make a better impression on others.

Writetype: Personality Types and Writing Styles (HRD Press, June 1994)

Based on individual personality styles, this book provides new strategies for the four basic types of writers: the correspondent, the technical writer, the creative writer, and the analytical writer. Each person fits one of these well-defined writing "types." Once readers learn their writing personality and follow the writing process suggested in the book, they find writing easier and less anxiety-producing.

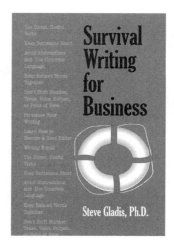

Survival Writing for Business (HRD Press, May 2005)

To write well, you need to keep it clear and concise. This book shows how and is a no-nonsense, a virtual lifeline to writing success.

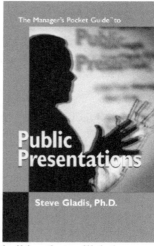

The Manager's Pocket Guide to Public Presentations (HRD Press, March 1999)

This book is an indispensable reference for managers and executives who find themselves in the unfamiliar and often frightening position of having to give a public presentation. It is a compendium of tips that will help any manager learn the survival tactics of public speaking. A simple, quick read, based on the accepted theory and practice of rhetoric, it is also a confidence builder that will help any manager begin to overcome anxiety over public speaking.